THE ULTIMATE
BOOK OF
HORSE BITS

SECOND EDITION

THE ULTIMATE
BOOK OF
HORSE BITS

SECOND EDITION

WHAT THEY ARE, WHAT THEY DO, AND HOW THEY WORK

Emily Esterson

Skyhorse Publishing

Skyhorse Publishing books may be purchased in bulk at special discounts for sales promotion, corporate gifts, fund-raising, or educational purposes. Special editions can also be created to specifications. For details, contact the Special Sales Department, Skyhorse Publishing, 307 West 36th Street, 11th Floor, New York, NY 10018 or info@skyhorsepublishing.com.

Skyhorse® and Skyhorse Publishing® are registered trademarks of Skyhorse Publishing, Inc.®, a Delaware corporation.

Visit our website at www.skyhorsepublishing.com.

10 9 8 7 6 5 4 3 2 1

Paperback ISBN: 978-1-5107-3883-6
ebook ISBN: 978-1-5107-3884-3

Library of Congress Cataloging-in-Publication Data is available on file.

Printed in China

TO VOLARE,
MY DREAM HORSE

1988–2009

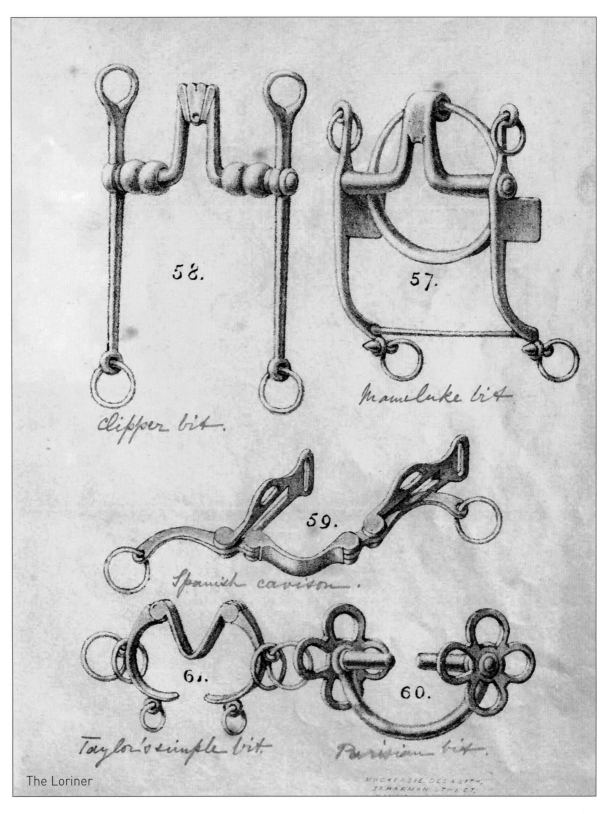

58. clipper bit.

57. Mameluke bit.

59. Spanish cavison.

61. Taylor's simple bit.

60. Parisian bit.

The Loriner

"I frequently tell my friends that out of every twenty bits I make, nineteen are for men's heads and not more than one really for the horse's head."
—Benjamin Latchford

CONTENTS

ACKNOWLEDGMENTS

Thank you!

Never for a minute have I wondered about the unique attributes of the equestrian community. But when you embark on a project such as this, you realize just how special your "horse friends" really are.

A tremendous thank you to Teun Van Riel of Equine Industry in the Netherlands. I visited Teun's mobile tack shop long before I actually met him, but it was clear to me that whoever owned that operation had a "thing about bits." Teun and his team graciously sent me photos of their Trust Bit series to illustrate the book and also answered my bit questions patiently and with grace.

Intrepid International also provided a great number of photos. My undying gratitude to John Craven for his enthusiasm about this project, for his contacts, for his knowledge, and for his friendship. John passed away in 2017, and his loss is felt deeply in the equestrian community. John, Larry Mitton (president of Intrepid), and Jeri Harris (who spent a day uploading a really long and rather annoying list of photos) all helped and you'll find many of Intrepid's products in the pages of this work.

Brigitte Schulte and Heinz Baumann gave me a tour of the Sprenger bit factory in Germany. Sprenger also helped out with photos and Brigitte took me out for a fabulous lunch, forever changing my opinion of German food.

My local community of horse people and their various boxes of bits, stories, anecdotes, and pearls of wisdom were all super helpful. Greg from Western Mercantile, which sadly closed its doors before this edition was published, and Melanie from Dan's Boots and Saddles lent me their inventory to photograph; Nancy Ambrosiano and Laura Simpson both let me photograph their bit collections and talked to me about bitting.

My veterinarians at the time I wrote this book, Mark Meddleton and Benoit Bouchet at Meddleton Equine, patiently answered my questions (always). They also allowed me (and Kip Malone) to chase them around with a camera.

Gracious photographer friends helped me fill in the blanks with their great work. Arnd Bronkhorst, John Brasseaux, Dusty

Perin, and Kip Malone all contributed work to the project.

Karan Miller of *Western Horseman* faxed me articles the magazine had run; I also gathered info from Juli Thorson at *Horse & Rider*. There were many conversations, both casual and formal, about the material contained herein.

To my readers—Scot Key, dear husband who knows nothing about bits but nevertheless continued to tell me to soldier on in my darkest hours, and Nicole Polligkeit, my trainer and friend—who read the book and made notes, corrected things, and basically improved it overall.

Two wonderful horses who modeled for this project passed away this year and will be forever missed. RosenKönig owned by my friends Wanda and Mark Hage of Paradigm Sport Horses in Los Lunas, New Mexico, was the gentlest soul of a black stallion and appears in several of the double bridle photos. Volare, my own beloved horse, is seen in the shot of a horse who hangs his tongue. This book is dedicated to them.

And to my other models, Baleno and Belle, who put up with wearing too big bits and too small bits, rope halters and bitless bridles; had fingers stuck in their mouths and their lips pulled back; and suffered through this project. They were paid handsomely in unconditional love and carrots.

ix

THE ULTIMATE
BOOK OF
HORSE BITS

CHAPTER - 1

SO MANY BITS

"I have always found in my long experience that the horse's mouth and temper may be compared to a lock, so made, that only one key will fit it; and to find the right bit patience and perseverance are necessary in so doing."

— Benjamin Latchford

When I walked into Teun Van Riel's horse van-turned-mobile tack store during the German Young Horse Championships in Warendorf, Germany, I knew right then what a project writing a book about bits was going to be.

I had just gotten the contract for this book based on an article I had written for the United States Equestrian Federation's magazine, *Equestrian*. As a way to begin my research, I'd started taking photos of any and all bits I came across. But in Van Riel's mobile tack store, I became overwhelmed with questions, all of which led back to one fundamental issue: How does one choose?

I certainly was no expert when I began this journey. Although I understood the basics of training and the purpose of bits, I didn't have any more knowledge than the slightly above average amateur. While writing the article for *Equestrian*, I had disabused myself of some of the things I'd heard about

bits during a lifetime of riding. I "knew," for example, that a snaffle is a soft bit and a curb a more severe bit (which turns out not always to be true). I didn't know why, or that there are a million nuances that disprove those two statements. In my personal collection were three or four double-jointed snaffles, a mullen-mouth, and a single gag bit purchased long ago for a horse that liked to take over on the cross-country course. The gag was recommended by a trainer and I had purchased and used it with much trepidation. I didn't understand how it worked, and in retrospect I probably shouldn't have been using it. I also had a couple of what are now considered old-fashioned single-jointed

At the Bundeschampionat in Warendorf, Germany, I found Equine Industry's mobile tack store. It was wall-to-wall bits.

snaffles—one eggbutt and one full cheek— that I've had for at least three decades.

So I came to this project relatively ignorant of my subject matter. To make it that much more challenging, I decided that I needed to make this book as broad as possible, encompassing as much of the bitting universe as I could. As a long-time English rider who started out in the jumper ring, moved to eventing, and is now trundling around the dressage arena, I knew little about Western bits and riding. I had a very judgmental attitude about those giant curb and spade bits I saw in Western horses' mouths, because they looked to me like instruments of torture.

Little did I know . . .

The Dutchman Van Riel described himself as a "bit obsessive," and indeed, if you talk to Europeans about bits three names come up: Hilary Vernon of Abbey Saddlery in the U.K., Heinz Baumann from Herm Sprenger in Germany, and Teun Van Riel from the Netherlands. At the Young Horse Championships, his mobile tack store was a museum of modern-day bits. He keeps hundreds of bits in inventory. And it's a stunning snapshot of just how vast and complicated the world of horse bitting is. For every traditional single-jointed snaffle bit on his pegboard wall, there was a unique design or a gadget-like addition. There were bits with rope mouthpieces, bits with lozenges of different sizes, bits with rollers, bits with a figure-eight in the center, bits with multiple links, bits made of German silver, bits made of sweet iron, bits made of plastic mounted on ropes, bits with a three-inch rotating ring in the center. There was a certain delightful beauty in the bit wall and I probably took a hundred photos of his inventory. He didn't have any Western bits, but I ran into several bit makers and suppliers later in my research that could rival him in terms of sheer quantity of inventory. They had snaffles; curbs with shanks of different lengths, ornate and simple; curbs with ports of varying heights and widths. You name it, they had it. Even our small local mercantile has plenty of Western bit inventory.

I've come to appreciate Van Riel's obsession. Since starting this project, I've purchased several new bits, but I've also started examining bits much more closely. Even on casual trips to the local feed store, I'm in the bit aisle feeling the cool metal, laying the bit over my hand to gauge its balance, rubbing the edges and moving parts to determine whether or not they have sharp edges.

One thing I've learned about bits is that having a lot of them doesn't necessarily solve your bit-related problems. It may save you money eventually because you can experiment with different options without forking over $50 to $100 (for quality) or more for a bit every time you want to try something new. But in the long run, problem solving takes skill, training, and thoughtfulness, not equipment. For many years, I owned an

Herm Sprenger GmbH has been making bits in Iserlohn, Germany, since the 1800s.

event horse that hung his tongue out of his mouth. It was a habit that started long before he came to me. In fact, he'd been doing it since he was born, and although there's no science documenting that tongue hanging is hereditary, his brother also had been known to hang his tongue.

You would think that I would have learned something about bitting during the sixteen years that I owned him. After all, every instructor I encountered just *had* to try to fix it. I tried special nosebands and tongue depressors and stuffing his mouth with peanut butter right before going into the dressage arena. I heard an astonishing number of rather cruel suggestions as to how to fix it: tie it down, cut it off, crank the noseband so tightly that the tongue can't stick out and the noseband leaves a dent in his chin. None of it ever helped. Volare's tongue habit stuck with him from birth to death, in January 2009 at the age of twenty-one.

It was just a few months after Volare died that my young horse decided that I was destined to learn even more about bitting and mouth problems by sticking her own tongue out of the left side of her mouth. I was right in the middle of my research for this book. I felt cursed, and yet blessed. Here was an opportunity to solve the tongue problem, using my newfound bitting knowledge. Turn to chapter 11 to see what happened.

Right now, there are thousands of different bits on the market at any given time. For each bit that's currently for sale, there's probably a new bit under development. And you can't deny that some of this proliferation in bit choices is a result of the marketing machine—the desire of bit makers to sell more products or for horse trainers to supplement their incomes with their own signature lines of bits. After all, how many double-jointed snaffles and variations does one need?

As it turns out, you can try many different bits and never quite find the right one. And two handcrafted bits that look identical can feel vastly different in the horse's mouth. It is one of the most sensitive parts of his body, able to pull a tiny sprout of grass delicately from beneath the dirt and direct it into his stomach. And as we learn more and more about the horse's anatomy thanks to science's advances, we're better able to determine how individual horses react to bits and what happens in their mouths when they are wearing bits.

During a visit to the Herm Sprenger bit factory in central Germany, where they have been making metal products for horses since the 1880s, Brigitte Schulte and Heinz Bauman, director of marketing and product developer, respectively, told me that designing bits wasn't just a market demand process (dressage rider Lisa Wilcox needs a new bit!)—it was a process of innovation. Sprenger has relationships with Germany's veterinary universities and is actually able to perform some research studies related to how bits work, what makes horses perform better in certain kinds of bits, and the materials that seem to suit horses' mouths. In fact, they are almost always working on new bits, whether for an upcoming catalogue or because one of the world's elite riders has

5

contacted them for help with a particular bitting problem—a common occurrence (and yes, there is now a Lisa Wilcox WH Ultra from Sprenger).

Nonetheless, bit-making is a business and has been since the very first loriners (bit makers) invented a new design for better battlefield control. Today, bit companies keep us buying by producing what could be the latest and greatest new tool to hit the market since we stopped using bones and ropes in our horses' mouths. And maybe because we don't know enough about training, or aren't as educated riders as we should be, we're convinced that the next bit will be the one to solve our problems.

Add in the fact that bits come in and out of style, just as certain styles of nosebands, saddles, pads, and everything else change according to whims of fashion. Some of these trends have been very, very useful to the horse and rider. Some have not. And for every "great new bit" there's someone who will tell you it's not worth the metal it was made of.

Fundamentally, all bits have the same purpose: to allow us to control our horses better. But when you dig deeper into bit theory, you can see all the small issues that can affect bit choice: the size of the horse's mouth, the thickness of his tongue, how high or low the palate is, the width and depth of the bars, the horse's training, his way of

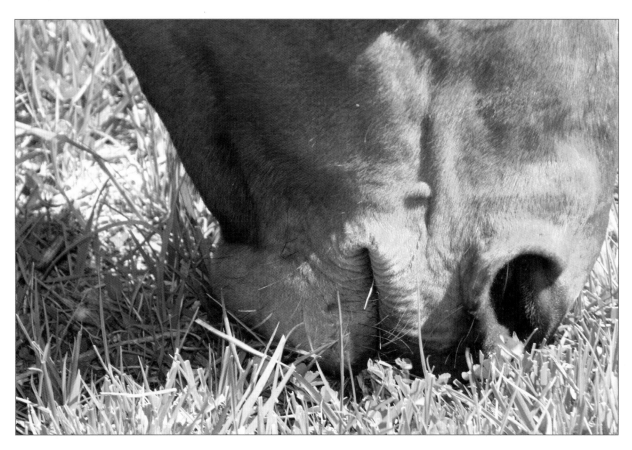

The horse's delicate and sensitive lips are designed to find food no matter the conditions.

going, his taste preferences (some horses love sweet iron; some don't), how he reacts to the bridle, and how it is adjusted. His conformation, his habits, and even the fit of his tack have an impact on which bit to choose and how to use it.

The manufacturers, too, incorporate subtle differences into their bits; a stainless steel simple D-ring snaffle may look the same from one catalog to the next, but manufacturers are rarely able to produce identical products from two different factories. As we know, horses are highly sensitive creatures and that stainless D-ring from X Company may have a slightly different weight or balance than the one from Y Company. It's quite possible, with a magnifying glass and close examination, you'll find an almost imperceptible difference between seemingly identical products.

And then there is the rider: How sensitive is he? How correct are his aids?

Has he trained the horse effectively, using knowledge of the scale of training for his chosen discipline? What's the difference between a Western horse's training and that of a dressage horse? Can a horse really feel differently in two bits that seem identical? What if the horse gets used to one bit and then doesn't respond as well? How does the bit figure in to the overall happy horse equation? Or should it at all?

The variables are mind-boggling.

Still, it's hard to imagine needing some of those more obscure items on Van Riel's bit wall. And, for the average amateur horse owner, there's probably no need for a silver dollar–sized lozenge on an oversized loose ring. Yet exploring some of the intricacies of bit design can bring us a great deal of insight into how the bit should work, what our horses' mouths are like, and how to use a bit humanely and wisely in concert with correct training. That, fundamentally, is the goal of this book.

7

CHAPTER - 2

IN THE BEGINNING

The museums of the world are full of bits. From simple bronze-age single-jointed snaffles, turned green with age and frequently found displayed alongside accoutrements of early Chinese and Mongol warriors, to Henry the VII's sixteenth-century curb bit with high port, players, balls, and rollers—a bit so elaborate it's more a piece of artwork than a riding tool. No matter the style—what's clear is that the ability to control a horse from his back has been an important part of humankind's development for a very long time.

THE DOMESTICATION OF THE HORSE

The first bits are said to have appeared in early pre-Roman times, circa 3500 BC, although archaeologists believe riding began as early as 4000 BC or even earlier, predating the development of the wheel. Before 4000 BC, horses appeared in cave paintings, but were probably hunted for meat rather than used for transportation and labor.

According to equine archaeological specialist David W. Anthony and his colleagues, the earliest major horse-related archaeological find appears at Dereivka, in what is now the Ukraine in the area south of Kiev. The people here practiced agriculture, and the number of horse bones in the refuse and burial pits is about twice what is found in other similar finds. A second area of horse domestication is located in two sites of the Botai, located in what is today northern Kazakhstan, dated about 3500 to 3000 BC. Eneolithic Botai culture thrived between 3100 and 3700, and archaeologists found evidence of mare's milk in bowls as well as other signs of domestication in the pit house communities they found there. It's likely that horses had been hunted as prey prior to this time, but with the discovery of some skeletal remains with clear tooth wear, archaeologists posited that the Botai had graduated from eating horses to using them for agricultural pursuits—or at least some of them, anyway.

The Botai site showed researchers how bit wear—even from "natural" bits, such as rope—can affect the teeth. There is no direct evidence of bits, since metal bits had not yet been invented and any rawhide or other soft material rotted into oblivion. But the Botai people moved heavy items, such as boulders, long distances. That suggests that they probably used horses (kept in corrals adjacent to their homes) as pack animals. A study conducted in 1992 by Anthony and Dorcas Brown on the Botai horses studied wear patterns on teeth of early Botai skeletal remains. They examined thirty-six sets of premolars from horse remains of different ages. The wear patterns suggest the use of a bit, although the true changes in horses' teeth patterns and evidence of bridling came much later.

Some scientists theorize that horses became domesticated in much the same way dogs did—in a symbiotic relationship wherein both parties realized the benefits of having the other around. While there's little clear evidence of this, it would be difficult to domesticate the horse without some cooperation on his part. It might have been that farmers tracked harem bands that followed regular paths and were able to find ways to corral them. It may be that older, slower, or infirm horses were the first domesticates. We can postulate that those horses that were easy to handle were bred, and bred again, leaving those who were not to forage on the steppes and be hunted for meat. During this same period, man was abandoning his hunter-gatherer lifestyle for a more staid, agricultural existence. As he planted and grew crops, horses became more and more necessary as pack animals and as traction to move items around the farm, although the cart had not yet been invented. The diminishing game herds close to their settlements forced these evolving bronze-age hunters to travel for their meat. Hence the riding horse and the bit were born.

However it happened, man and horse alike found value in their mutually beneficial relationship and the world changed significantly.

THE FIRST BITS

Much of what we know about the bridling and bitting of horses in ancient times comes from the art and artifacts that have been dug up. For the most part, skin-based saddlery disintegrates, so there's little left of ancient harness work, but archaeologists have found depictions of horses and other equids partaking in various activities such as plowing, pulling chariots, and being ridden. Horses didn't appear in the Middle East until around 2200 BC, although people in this region had already been using asses for draft work. Through close examination of the archaeological record we are able to, more or less, recreate the horse's early uses and training. For example, horses are depicted in the Standard of Ur, an ancient box from Sumeria (modern-day Iraq) that dates from around 2600 BC. The box is covered in an elaborate mosaic depicting war and peace. Here, horselike animals pull wagons and

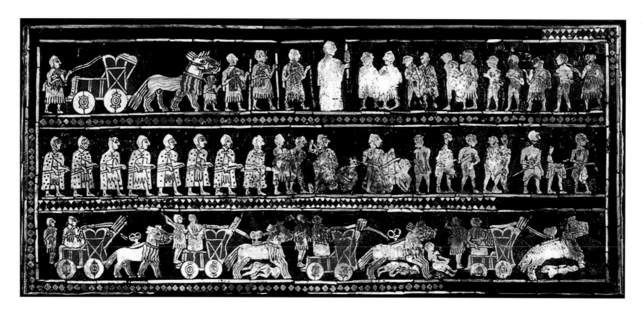

Our understanding of ancient horsemanship comes primarily from the depiction of horses in art and archeological finds. The Standard of Ur is from Sumeria (modern day Iraq), dating from 2600 BC. It depicts horses and their harnesses as used in warfare.

10

chariots, clearly wearing a round-ringed bit device—possibly even a ring through their noses.

Of course, the very first bits were made before the development of metals, using materials that were close at hand, such as hemp rope, bone, horn, or hard wood. Antlers with holes drilled through them for rope appear to be the first real bit, although we can't be sure.

When man learned to mine iron out of the earth and smelt it with tin to create bronze, another age of horseback riding began. The horse became widely used for warfare, sport (chariot racing), and agriculture. In some early finds, horses' remains have been found buried with chariots, bridlework, and human bodies, which gives us some inkling of the importance that horses had gained since their early days as an animal hunted for meat. Art from ancient Egypt, Mesopotamia,

and Greece, as well as from China, depicts ornate bridle and harness work; already man's understanding of horse training had evolved beyond just using an ox harness or nose ring to a more sophisticated training and steering system—a device in the mouth attached to some form of rope from which the rider or driver controls the horse's head. In excavations of the Dereivka, archaeologists found long, slender pieces of antler that had holes in them. These were most likely the first "full cheek" cheek pieces ever invented. Shaped like a half-moon, the antler piece would have applied cheek pressure and bar and tongue pressure simultaneously.

THE WAR HORSE

What happened next? The horse's use evolved as man changed. Greek bas reliefs circa 900 BC show evidence of horses being used to pull chariots. They did not wear a cavesson, but instead were guided by a rope in the mouth. Early Indo-Aryans, Mongols, and Chinese were the first serious inventors of bits, the designs of which remain in use today. Museum collections contain simple, single-jointed snaffles made of bronze that look like they could be found in tack stores today.

Enter the chariot: In the classic movie *Ben Hur*, a chariot race scene is one of the most anxiety-filled for any horse lover. The wildness of the race scene and the use of the chariot as a weapon to dislodge the competitors, although colorized by Hollywood's fine set of paints, was nonetheless a somewhat accurate depiction of the use of horses during the Roman Empire. The horse's use during that time was as just another piece of weaponry. The Romans employed the weight of their animals and their chariots to trample and upset enemies.

Horse and chariot warriors, however, faced some problems. The reins of the original "bits," or steering devices, went back through the harness and allowed the drivers to exert leverage on the horse's mouth to stop the forward motion—but that's all. They really had no steering to speak of. Charioteers wrapped the reins around their waists and leaned their body weight to influence their galloping chariot horses while holding a whip in one hand. Archaeological records show that bits during ancient Greek chariot races had straight bars. Drivers put the strongest horse on the outside of the team so he'd be able to turn the vehicle.

Experts postulate that the curb bit appeared in the fourth century BC, most likely an invention of the Celts. The leverage action of the curb provided a great deal more control for warfare—the primary use of the horse at that time—and allowed the horse-

Although fictional, the movie *Ben Hur* factually depicted the use of horse and chariot for sport in Roman times.

revering people a canvas on which to express their coat of arms or affiliations. The addition of the long shanks, often carved or endowed with royal crests, allowed for an incredible military advantage and may have allowed the Celts to earn their reputation as warring barbarians. They actually attempted to sack Rome but were driven back to their territory on the northern side of the Alps.

As horses from different areas interbred, their sizes and shapes changed. As they ate more and grew larger and more powerful, the need to control them became a foremost military effort. Bits turned from benign to barbaric in a matter of a few years, although they also evolved aesthetically at the same time. The ornamentation and complexity of the decoration of that time serve as models for the craftsmanship we know today in Western bits.

Examples of early bits show an innate understanding of equine nature: The cheek pieces were adorned with all manner of spikes and pegs and other devices to encourage the horse to turn away from pressure. Unfortunately, bit makers invented devices that would inflict pain when the bit came in contact with the horse's cheeks. Nonetheless, there were a few "aha" moments in horse training: It was acknowledged that a horse who kept his head down and his poll flexed was easier to control. A more balanced seat was also coming into fashion. It was around this time that the martingale and draw reins were invented to keep the horse's head down, allowing more control.

The greatest horsemen of the ancient world were warriors, first and foremost. It was a tough world back then—a kill-or-be-killed type of environment. Bits of the last few centuries BC reflected man's need to be tough in battle, and the need for the warrior to be able to maneuver quickly with minimal wasted movement. Those bits can be viewed today with particular disdain from our viewpoint of "natural horsemanship." Nonetheless, such devices paved the way for the Egyptians, Celts, and Romans to become great ancient warriors of their times.

THE AGE OF XENOPHON

Xenophon's *The Art of Horsemanship*, which appeared around 350 BC, was the first writing on horsemanship that advocated gentler riding methods. As he explains in the chapter on how to make a horse more magnificent and striking, "You must refrain from pulling on the bit." While we hear that all the time today, remember that back then riders knew no other method of controlling their horses. Xenophon goes so far as to recommend that every horseman should have two bits: one smooth with disks of good size and the "other with the disks heavy and not standing so high, but with the *echini* sharp so when he seizes it, he may drop it from dislike of its roughness."

Xenophon was a Greek historian who lived from 430–354 BC. His work *The Art of Horsemanship* describes the proper use of bits. He believed they should be used in conjunction with a well-developed and balanced seat, not as the sole form of control. He was well ahead of his time.

In his writing, Xenophon clearly advocates what we know to be true about horse anatomy, natural behavior, and the influence of having a human on his back. "The horse's mouth must not be checked too harshly so that he will toss his head, nor too gently for him to feel it."

Hence, what we advocate as a soft, conversational contact with the bit is indeed what Xenophon discovered in 350 BC. Xenophon is required reading for the serious horseman.

THE MEDIEVAL PERIOD TO THE MODERN ERA

Over the next centuries, horseback riding and the equipment used to control horses evolved substantially. If you look closely at bits from the medieval period, when horses were integrated into culture for work, sport, and warfare, many of the same bits that were in use back then are still in use today. In fact, in his 1940 study of ancient bits, Oxford historian John Bryan Ward Perkins called the variety "bewildering . . . it is hardly possible to do more than indicate the commoner forms and the approximate period of their use." The main differences between the bit styles of the Middle Ages and today is ornamentation, Ward Perkins writes. The knights were fond of highly ornamental cheek pieces. Ward Perkins doesn't identify the two kinds of bits, but it's obvious from his descriptions that he's talking about the curb and the snaffle. The curb bit uses indirect rein contact with the bit to control the horse. The snaffle is a direct contact bit: pull on the

reins and the horse feels the pressure directly on his mouth. The monograph notes that there were five common cheek pieces and six common mouthpieces. The cheek pieces were a ring, a ring with bars coming out of the ring's center top and bottom, a full cheek with a D-shaped ring, a full cheek with thick bars, and a type we don't see much today—a ring with two C's pointed backwards. This double C would serve a similar purpose as the full cheek; however, depending on the configuration, the points of the C's (which are rounded) would cause more widely distributed pressure on the cheeks.

Mouthpieces from Ward Perkins's collection are fairly straightforward: a straight bar, a single-jointed bit, a double-jointed bit with the center segment made of a wire loop, a single-jointed snaffle made with two hollow cones (the predecessor of today's hollow mouth), a single-jointed ported bit, and a curb with a rather high port.

The fifteenth and sixteenth centuries were truly the eras of bit ingenuity. Most stable managers were still convinced that it was by the bit alone that a rider could get his horse to submit to his will, but they also began to understand that horses reacted differently to different bits, so they began to experiment. During this period, bit makers became true artisans who were able to combine mouthpieces with cheeks and offer riders some of the variety that we have today. Federico Grisone, for example, was a sixteenth-century Italian said to be a master of dressage education. Grisone published one of the most read Renaissance manuals of horsemanship, *The Orders of Horsemanship,*

ORDINI

DI CAVALCARE

DI FEDERIGO GRISONE

Gentil'huomo Napoletano.

LIBRO PRIMO.

ELL'ARTE della Milia
tia non è disciplina di maggior
bellezza di questa de i Caual=
li, & non che ornata di belli ef=
fetti : mà necessaria, & uestita
d'ogni ualore, et tanto è più dif
ficile, & degna di lode, quanto
in essa ui bisogna usar il tempo, & la misura, & più, &
meno l'uno, & l'altro mancar, & accrescere col uero, et
buon discorso, tal che anchora il senso dell'udire, & del
uedere, nó hauendo la pratica regolata dall'intelletto ui

Sixteenth-century Italian equitation master Federico Grisone's *Ordini di Cavalcare* encouraged the use of harsher bits to control horses.

during that time. Although Grisone did use some of Xenophon's theories, he believed in harsher methods to obtain submission, and the bits he invented reflect it. Horse trainers of the day still believed in force and pain, and the bit was a major weapon in their arsenal.

Some of the ingenious creations of that time included telescoping shanks and a variety of "players" for the tongue, including balls that spun, keys that dangled, and olive-shaped mouthpieces. One bit had a ball, a solid oval with a drilled center, a center ring resembling today's Dick Christian, and three or four keys hanging off the center. The philosophy seemed to be, "the more stuff on the mouthpiece, the better." For the most part, the shanks were impossibly long—300 to 400 millimeters (11 to 15 inches). The length of the shanks caused the ends to splay apart, so bit makers added a bar or chain toward the bottom of the shank (called "hobbles" today) to connect them. This also helped the rider who needed to control his horse with one hand, because the strap made the shanks, and their action on the mouthpiece, work in concert. In addition to the great length of the shanks, the bits of the day were also quite heavy: many weighed as much as 800 grams, or about 30 ounces. Bits were still primarily made of bronze or iron; it wasn't until significant metallurgical experimentation in the twentieth century that bits appeared in different materials.

An antique curb bit shows the severity of some of the ports on older bits.

The Spanish Spade and Mikmar: Note the similarities.

Besides the excessive lengths of the shanks, the difference between the curbs of the Renaissance and today is that the ports were much higher. Historians theorize that such elaborate long-shanked bits were really for show. Working horses, plow horses, and other "regular" horses were ridden and driven in snaffles, as evidenced by the number of snaffle bits found in archaeological sites. Still, there are plenty of paintings that depict the working horse with a rope halter and a curb bit. Historians chalk this up to artist interpretation rather than veracity.

The seventeenth century saw diminishment in the diversity of bits and the customized fashion in which they were made. Xenophon's balanced seat philosophy had finally taken hold. Horsemanship evolved from using the bit for control to the use of the seat and aids. The great French equestrian, Antoine du Pluvinel,

instructor to Louis the XIII, was known for his humane training methods, and as such was able to influence equestrianism in significant ways, not the least of which was to diminish the popularity of the spiked, sharp, and inhumane bits that predated him. Du Pluvinel's legacy is clearly seen today: he advocated refining the horse's training to the point where just the very lightest touch on a simple curb bit had an influence on the horse. He was one of the first proponents of gentle horse-training methods.

Almost all the bits of today are only variations on former themes. From the Middle Ages to the Industrial Revolution, nothing much changed about bits—curbs and jointed snaffles ruled the day. We still have five or six mouthpieces and five or six styles of cheeks. Even hackamores, bitless bridles, and rope halters have their origins in early equestrianism. The Spanish vaqueros (cowboys) trained their horses in a *jaquima* (hackamore) before adding a bit—a practice brought to the Americas by the Spanish Conquistadors who also left a few horses behind. Loriners of yesterday are much the same as those of today, crafting bits based on style or perceived need. Compare photos of a seventeenth-century Spanish spade bit, for example, to a Mikmar from 2009: the mouthpiece is wide, the port is smooth, the entire apparatus lies back on the tongue. With the exception of ornamentation, the bits are nearly identical. Check out the Arms and Armor exhibition at the Metropolitan Museum of Art in New York City. There in the case with the Mongol warrior is a single-jointed snaffle bit that could be found in any tack store today.

THE ARRIVAL OF THE BIT IN NORTH AMERICA

No matter what style of riding you practice, be assured that your bit's origins came from Europe. One clear example is the Western spade bit, with slightly shorter shanks, a very wide mouthpiece, and a large spade that curves back against the tongue. After all, there were no horses on the North American continent until the conquistadors brought them here. No matter the differences between Western and English, all our U.S. equestrianism evolved from the same basic place: the military battlefield of the Middle Ages.

While avid riders might be righteous about their particular training methods and their discipline's "better way," such argument

is largely moot. Everything we know about horse training has come originally from the ancient battlefields of Europe, Asia, and the Middle East. Horses had to learn to jump obstacles with riders aboard during battle. They moved sideways, forward, and backward, leaping up and kicking out behind. Today you can see such high-level training in the mounted police forces, during the performance of the Lipizzaner horses, and in the dressage and jumper show rings. These types of riding may look far-flung from the cow horse working on the ranch in Montana, but their origins—and their equipment—at one time were identical.

When the Spanish conquistadors came to this country through the seventeenth century, they brought with them the skills and the basic equipment of European equestrianism. They were granted large tracts of land in the region we now know as California, becoming known as the "californio" ranches. They were famous for the length of time they took to finish their highly refined reining horses. Their classical training method involved starting their horses in a hackamore or rope bitless bridle that applied pressure on the nose and the poll for control. Technically, the word "bosal" refers to the noseband of such a bridle, but it is common today to use the expression "bosal hackamore" when describing a specific type of rope bitless bridle (see chapter 10).

As the horse was trained, the vaqueros gradually added first a light snaffle with two reins, then a curb-style bit, and finally the spade bit. The spade bit required the lightest of hands and the lightest trained horse to achieve the classic forward vaquero reining horse. The vaquero used a romal rein, which was heavy enough and the bit quick enough to transmit the minutest signal. The horses of the day were lighter in build and smaller, and when tackling the chores of a working cowboy the vaquero's horse had to be delicately trained to move away or toward a cow in an instant.

No less refined, Texas-style horsemanship evolved from the same basic riding technique, but with a faster and harder rider. He was more apt to use a grazer bit with a much lower port and turned back, solid shanks. The Texas cowboy didn't need as much lateral flexibility, and was riding a larger, fleeter horse bred to chase cows. The grazer bit's shanks curved back to allow the horse to graze during long days working cattle on the ranch.

The difference in control between Texas and vaquero training styles was the result of the time it took to "finish" a horse, and the practicalities of the horse's use. For example, the finished reining horse in the vaquero tradition was controlled with subtle movements of the left hand, positioned further back than the cow horse rider's hand. The severity of the bit also required additional equipment to keep it even, light, and soft in the hand. The reins were made of braided rawhide to keep them from swinging and causing extra motion against the bit, aided even more by the addition of chains to the end of the reins. Many of today's romal

reins have safety catches to release should the rein catch on something.

The Texas cowboy, on the other hand, was more likely to neck rein with the hand forward in front of the horn. The reins were light and split, and the bit was less adorned. The working cowboy spent hours on the range. When not in pursuit of an errant cow, the cowboy's horse walked forward with his head and neck low, and the cowboy rode with a passive hand and a relaxed position. But when the action heated up (such as when a cow took flight or the cowboy needed to rope a steer), the rider took up more contact, raised his hand, and came forward a bit in the saddle to be able to maneuver his cows and his horse quickly.

Throughout history, the need for control of horses in warfare drove extensive innovation in bit design, producing a variety of styles over the centuries, from Ancient Greece into modern-day use. A browse through museum display cases confirms that while we certainly know a great deal more about horses and riding than we did in 3000 BC, our bit styling has not changed drastically since those early attempts at controlling horses.

History and tradition are part of equestrianism. They are among the many reasons that we love the sport and art of riding. Our bits, despite our ability to fashion new metals and better understand our horses through science and observation, remain largely unchanged.

19

CHAPTER - 3

ANATOMY OF THE MOUTH

The horse's mouth and head are well designed for carrying a bit. The bit itself sits on the bars of the mouth. When a bit moves, it makes contact with a number of pressure points that vary according to the type of bit, the way the bit is attached to the bridle, and the fit of the bridle as well as the bit. The pressure points range from minimal to acute. The choice of bit very much depends upon which pressure points are most important for the rider to accomplish his riding and training goals, and upon the preferences of the horse and his way of going.

Those pressure points are:

- Poll
- Tongue
- Lips
- Palate
- Bars
- Chin groove
- Nose

To understand how bitting developed and how it functions today, it helps to understand the horse's functional anatomy. Early horses' teeth and mouth structures were similar to those of today's horses. Eohippus—the horse thought to be the predecessor of modern equines—was a smaller animal, and so it had fewer teeth and a shallower jaw line. Mesohippus, which lived 25 to 40 million years ago, developed with a gap between the front and back teeth as his face became more elongated.

Nature designed the horse's mouth for grazing in his sometimes harsh environment. The design of the horse's mouth and his agile lips allow him to move dirt aside to find the most nutritious forage. The process begins with the incisors, at the front of the mouth. The horse uses these teeth to grab and tear the grass out of the ground. Saliva is created once anything foreign enters the mouth cavity, which then softens the forage so it can be ground by the molars and prepared for digestion.

As it turns out, the anatomy of Equus callabus (the horse we know today) did us, their future domesticators, a great favor. The very convenient gap between the front incisors and the molars of the equine skull is the crucial structure for any and all discussions of proper bitting. This gap, called the bars, is in a perfect place for seating a bit.

We don't know how man came to figure out that the space between the molars and the incisors would make a good place to put a rope you could use to steer a horse, or that putting something in a horse's mouth and then using it to direct his head would ultimately make him a "rideable" horse. That question remains unanswered, just as we're not sure who and what events led early man to figure out that rubbing flint together would create fire. Both inventions were crucial to humankind's development.

At first glance, horses' heads look the same: soft nostrils, the slit of the lips, the whiskers. Look a little closer, however, and notice that every horse has a different mouth. Try the following experiment: Find three or four horses who will let you stick your fingers in their mouths. Take your index and second fingers and slide them gently into each horse's mouth at the bars, where the bit normally goes. Make a note of what you feel inside. Are you feeling the roof of the mouth? How much space is there between the top of the tongue and the palate? How wide is the horse's mouth? Now pull back his lips and measure how long the bars are. Are they the same on both sides? How much

Nature created a nice space for the bit—between the molars and the front incisors.

does the length of the bars differ from mouth to mouth? How do the teeth look? Are they the same as those of other horses? Then do the same experiment from the other side. What kinds of differences do you notice?

No doubt you'll find that each horse is different in some way; you'll also find that one side of a horse's mouth may be different from the other. You might also notice different colors in the horses' mouths—dark patches or bright pink or almost red spots. Peel back the lips and notice how the teeth fit together. Does each horse have the same bite?

Just like humans, only without the benefit of modern-day orthodontic treatment, horses have all kinds of different mouths. When I visited the Herm Sprenger bit factory in Germany, Heinz Baumann, who has been designing bits at Sprenger for decades, said he planned to become a bit fitter when he retired. Although he was half joking, Baumann's become something of that already, working with top European and American riders to build new bits for their problem horses. So why, then, aren't there more loriners who make bits specifically for your horse's mouth? After all, there are plenty of custom saddle makers in the world.

Besides being logical, if hideously expensive in today's production-based economy, having bits made to order would seem to solve many of the problems riders face with their mounts, especially considering how vastly different horses' mouths are. Unfortunately, custom bit makers would encounter many dissatisfied clients because the majority of bit problems are actually training problems.

Nonetheless, the individuality of the horse's mouth has been the subject of recent study by Sprenger's university partners as well as a number of U.S.-based veterinary researchers. Sprenger worked with the Hannover Anatomy Institute in Hannover, Germany, to determine how the width of the bit impacts the horse's mouth and how the position of the bit affects the anatomical structures of the mouth. They used a group of thirty-one three- and four-year-old horses. Researchers measured the distance between the bit and the palate both with the horses at rest and with rein contact. The study noted that the choice of the proper bit very much depends on the size of the horse's mouth, and that the old adage about thick bits being softer than thin ones may not apply to those horses with thick tongues and low palates. In that case, the thicker bit may be more severe and uncomfortable.

Continuing research has found that the distance between the tongue and the palate can vary as much as an inch between horses. The research has also found that horses can have as much as a 5 mm difference between the right and the left sides of their mouths.

Interestingly, these studies discovered that the size of the horse's mouth has little to no correlation to the size of the horse. The large horse does not necessarily have a large mouth. Anecdotally, my event horse, Volare, was 17.1 hands and wore an astonishingly large size 86 blanket. When it came to his head, though, he had a rather delicate jaw and muzzle; he wore a regular size 4¾-inch French link snaffle. Later I used his same bit on my delicately built, 15.2-hand filly.

While most bits today are made for what we can call a bell curve of horse sizes—where the majority wear a bit that ranges from 4½ inches to 5½ inches—several manufacturers are making smaller and larger bits that are fit proportionately. For many years, pony bits were just sized-down versions of horse bits, and the same was true for oversized draft bits. The better quality manufacturers, however, are resizing and re-proportioning their over- and under-sized bits to fit the larger and smaller mouths. Because of the sensitivity of your horse's jaw bones, tongue, and palate, it is not enough to buy a size 5 bit because that's what you think your horse will wear. You have to know how to hang that bit in his mouth, and how much room there should be between his lips and the bit ring. As such, measuring your bits and knowing how to tell when a bit fits properly is very important to your horse's comfort.

THE THROAT

Next time the equine dentist comes to call (which should happen twice a year, ideally), ask if you can put your arm inside the horse's mouth (obviously he should be nicely tranquilized and wearing a locked speculum). Your arm, depending on your size, will likely go in up to your elbow before reaching the back of the throat. Despite the astonishing length of a horse's mouth cavity, it is still possible for certain types of bits to interfere with both a horse's back teeth and his swallowing and breathing mechanisms.

Consider the horse's throat anatomy: To simplify what is a very complex system, there are two "pipes" in a horse's throat. One goes down the esophagus and the other down the trachea. The esophagus leads to the stomach while the trachea leads to the lungs. Unlike humans and dogs, who can breath either through their noses or their mouths, the horse breathes exclusively through his nose. Deep in the gullet, the soft palate opens and closes like a door when the horse swallows, allowing food to enter the esophagus. According to Dr. Robert Cook's studies of bitting, a horse can either breathe deeply or swallow, but it cannot do both at the same time.

A horse that's quietly grazing in the pasture has his mouth open while he eats. His nostrils take in and expel air, and his mouth is wet from saliva. He gathers up a lot of material before he swallows, hence the length of his mouth cavity. The tongue, one of the most important pieces of the bitting equation, is attached to the hyoid bones, which are attached to the jawbones. The hyoid bones are in the shape of the bottom half of a rectangular box deep in the throat, in which where the tongue rests. The hyoid bones prevent the tongue from dropping into the throat. The hyoid apparatus is compressed slightly when the poll is deeply flexed.

A study performed by researchers at the University of Michigan measured how a bit affects swallowing. Horses were wearing a bitless bridle, a jointed snaffle, or a Myler bit (see page 52) and had side reins attached for poll flexion. The researchers then measured the number of times the horses swallowed while cantering. None of the bits prevented swallowing, but horses did swallow less frequently in certain kinds of bits. The study also noted how having a bit in the horse's mouth creates different behaviors, from a quiet, closed mouth to using the tongue to raise the bit within the mouth.

Dr. Cook notes that placing a bit in a horse's mouth switches on his digestive system. When he takes something in his mouth, it stimulates his salivary reaction. Although some researchers believe it is the flexion of the horse's poll while bridled that compresses the parotid gland and stimulates salivation, causing the horse to wet his mouth in anticipation of food, others argue that putting anything in the mouth—bit, grass, or water—stimulates salivation. That, in turn, prepares the horse for swallowing by raising the soft palate so nothing gets into his airway.

SALIVATION

Some horses are much more sensitive about certain parts of their bodies—their polls, for example, may not tolerate the pressure of the bridle's crown piece. They may have sensitive ears, lips, or cheeks. They may prefer the taste of a certain metal over another metal. Like eighteenth-century loriner Benjamin Latchford wrote, there's a "key" for each horse's mouth. Finding what he likes will take a lot of experimentation and thoughtful riding.

The salivary glands provide the lubrication necessary to move food from the front of the mouth to the epiglottis, where swallowing takes place. The glands discharge the enzymatic fluid that helps the food break down. Salivation signals the digestive tract to get ready for food.

When a horse chews, it triggers the salivary glands to prepare the food for digestion and creates saliva. Introducing a bit—a foreign object in the mouth—creates the same response. Horses that are relaxed and happy in their bits will generally chew softly, creating a wet mouth, while those who are tense or tight may lock down on the bit and not create much saliva at all.

There is some controversy in the science about whether a soft, salivating mouth is necessary for a responsive horse—some horses simply don't chew when they have a bit in their mouths. Others slobber when they're upset or in ill health. In some equestrian disciplines the horse's chewing isn't necessarily a sign that they're well trained. In others it's considered a sign of relaxation and "acceptance" of the bit.

Dr. Cook notes that racehorses or other sport horses that bleed through the nose during exertion are actually being partially asphyxiated by their own tongues, which have drawn back in their mouths in retreat from the bit and in preparation for swallowing. In so doing, the root of the tongue cuts off the airway and causes partial asphyxiation.

Another problem horses face because of the tongue's relationship to the rest of the body is tension in the neck. Dr. Joyce Harman notes that the hyoid bones are actually the origination of the two most important neck muscles that attach to the sternum and the inside of the shoulder. Thus a tense tongue will cause a stiff horse.

Drs. Clayton, Manfredi, et al. note that the relationship between salivation and bit is difficult to pinpoint. Excessive salivation, they write, can actually be induced by the bit and exacerbated in some cases by a horse's inability to swallow often enough. Dr. Cook contends that salivation and a busy mouth can actually be signs of discomfort. In an effort to remove the bit from his mouth or move it away from an area of pain, he may be excessively busy with his mouth, chewing and fussing and playing.

What Clayton found goes against the common belief that bitting increases swallowing. The fact that swallowing frequency did not increase in the bitted horses versus those in bitless bridles or halters proves that salivation may actually be the result of another physiological action—flexion of the poll, for example. She concluded that the presence of a bit doesn't prevent swallowing when horses canter with flexed polls.

A soft mouth produces some foamy saliva.

THE MOUTH ITSELF

The inside of your horse's mouth is where most bits have an impact: the front teeth (incisors), the major palatine foramen (palate canal), and the bars of the mouth, which are the long spaces between the canines or tushes in male horses or the third incisors in females and the wolf teeth (if they are still present) or the molars. The bars become knife-edge sharp the closer you get to the front teeth.

Photo by: Kip Malone

A view of the incisors. This horse, despite being twelve years old, has not lost two of her baby teeth.

TEETH

Without going into too much detail about equine dentition (there are other books for that), the teeth and their proper care are key to comfortable bitting. Generally, male horses have canine teeth just behind the front incisors, but female horses may only have a small bump, if anything at all, in that

location. The bars are between that bump and the molars. This area should be smooth and uniform, running from three to four inches depending on the horse. The upper jaw has the same toothless area, but it is somewhat shorter in length than the lower jaw. An additional tooth sometimes grows just before the molars—it's a small, pointed tooth known as a wolf tooth. Not all horses develop them, but they can be quite sharp. Occasionally, they can also interfere with the bit or be irritating to the horse. No matter how well a bit fits a horse, there will always be some wearing on the teeth.

Equine archaeological specialist David W. Anthony and his colleagues, in trying to determine how to assess possible bit wear in the earliest horses, studied the premolars (the teeth closest to the bit) of both domestic and feral horses. They determined that horses that have been ridden with a bit have four clear types of tooth damage, even if they've been ridden with a rope or other natural material. The enamel of the first cuspid is scarred on the cheek, tongue, and front sides of the tooth. The teeth exhibit

small fractures on the surface and the movement of the bit over these fractures causes even more irregular damage. Lastly, the front of the tooth has been worn down. Given such a large amount of damage to the teeth, one can only imagine how an ill-fitting metal bit feels against the much more fragile structures of the tongue, the bars, and the lips.

If you compare the teeth of a horse that has never worn a bit and the teeth of one that has, you can quite easily see the results. The second and third premolars have likely become worn down. The more severe the rider's hands, the more wear on those sets of teeth. Keep this image in mind during our exploration of bits.

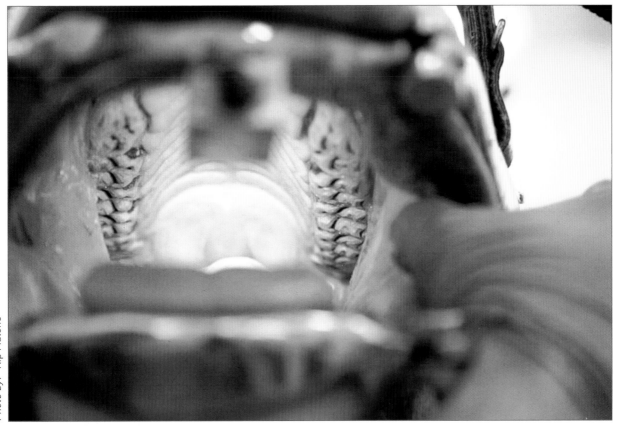

Photo by: Kip Malone

Looking in the horse's mouth, you can see the upper molars and the palate.

A dental care professional should examine your horse's jaw and his bite at least once a year. A poor bite, where the top and bottom teeth don't come together evenly, can make wearing a bit quite uncomfortable, or cause the horse to move his jaws side to side. It can also be the root of a tongue problem. While there are no orthodontics for horses, a veterinarian or equine dentist can shape the teeth so the jaws fit more evenly and repair a bite problem.

Like our own, horses' teeth change substantially over time, with an immature horse of three or four still losing his milk teeth, and a twenty-year-old horse having much more sloping teeth. In between, horses develop markings on their teeth that can help determine their age as well as their dental health. Understanding how horses' teeth and mouths change can help riders understand how important it is to consider different bit choices as their horses age in both chronological and training years.

SENSITIVE JAWS AND POLL

Besides varying in length, the horse's upper and lower jaws are different widths. The upper jaw is wider than the lower jaw, a fact

Photo by: Kip Malone

A dental care professional or properly trained veterinarian should examine your horse's teeth at least once a year. Here, Dr. Mark Meddleton of Meddleton Equine in Corrales, New Mexico, performs a thorough dental exam.

that may not have an impact on the actual bit choice, but may determine the size of the bit you choose. If you examine a horse with his mouth closed, you'll notice his upper lip is slightly wider than the lower one, reflecting his wider upper jaw. Also, the horse's jaws have basically no muscle—meaning there is no protection from pressure between the jaw bones and the nerves. Consider the feeling of metal on bone; that's what your horse feels from the bit. The nerves are close to the surface. Pressure is translated instantly from rein to brain. Additionally, the nerves residing in both upper hard and soft palates are relatively exposed, meaning that they, too, are highly sensitive to pressure and pain.

The anatomy of the horse's mouth is rather obvious: the bit goes in the space between the molars and the incisors, and rests on the tongue. The edges of the bit can press against the bars, the lips, and, depending on the type of bit, possibly the roof of the mouth (the palate).

The equine mouth and head are extremely sensitive, thanks to the location and sensitivity of the facial nerves. There are twelve cranial nerves that control many of the functions and senses, such as taste, sight, hearing, and touch. They are the same nerves that control a horse's chewing and salivation mechanisms. Both of those mechanisms, as well as swallowing and the flexion of the head and neck, are directly correlated to the pressure on the reins and the bit. The mouth, jaw, and lips are thin structures, and the nerves are quite close to the surface.

The trigeminal nerve—or C5—is probably most important in the equine head when it comes to bitting. This nerve originates at the pharynx, splits into three branches (hence *tri*geminal), and follows the length of the mouth both on the top and the bottom of jaw. The nerve commands sensation from the jaw; it also commands the muzzle, upper jaw, and nasal cavity. The trigeminal nerve is said to be responsible for much of the feeling in a horse's muzzle and mouth. It is, in essence, his facial command center.

Scientific studies note that these nerves are so sensitive they can react to light, even though they are under the skin (a condition that may be one cause of a chronic condition called head-shaking). Researchers have found that an ordinary rider with light hands exerts hundreds of pounds of pressure per square centimeter (or 0.15 inch) on the bit. The horse feels this pressure acutely in the trigeminal nerve upon which the bit is sitting.

Other areas of sensitivity are the corners of the horse's lips. The skin here is most sensitive, designed so that the horse can use his lips to find food in otherwise barren landscapes. His lips are like little radar antennas, with his whiskers helping out. A horse who has his whiskers shaved off for the first time may have difficulty finding his food. Watch a horse as he grazes in what appears to be a relatively unfertile pasture: he'll use his lips to gently wipe away the surface soils to expose the shoots of grass and other forages down below. This hypersensitivity is one of the ways horses were able to survive in the wild.

The horse's brain sits in a small "box" just behind the ears. The poll, a knobby point on the top of the horse's head, protects the brain

29

box and is also covered by the very thinnest layer of skin. When the rider takes a feel of the reins, the pressure on the bit radiates up the cheek pieces and over the top of the horse's poll via the bridle's crown piece. A horse ridden in a leverage bit, such as curb or other long-shanked bit, will feel more pressure on the poll than one ridden in a regular direct-pressure (snaffle) bit.

Everything about a horse's head— command central—is designed to be related to his "fight or flight" decision-making process. So when pressure is applied to the horse's head, he reacts by either yielding to or fighting against that pressure. A well-trained horse and rider pair have developed good communication, and the horse relaxes and accepts the bit.

When early bits were designed, man was most interested in training methods related to pain—early bits, as noted above, included spikes and harsh mouthpieces, largely because man didn't know any better. Today's bits, while certainly much more evolved, can have the same impact in the wrong hands. Xenophon's early wisdom stressed the use of leg aids and the seat as well as the very light hand. As noted, he was well ahead of his time.

Horses with ill-fitting or misused bits definitely show the signs of pain, many of which are misunderstood as training or "bad horse" issues. Injuries caused by bits can include ulcers forming on the bars, bruising, lacerations, or other signs of trauma. A look at a skull of a bitted horse shows the bone

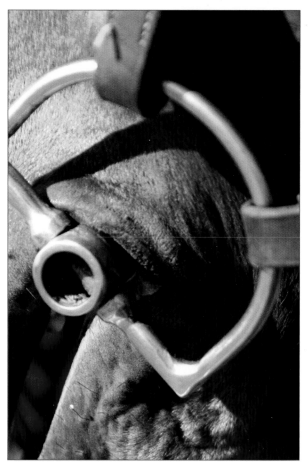

This horse cannot close his mouth over the bit, indicating that the mouthpiece is too thick for him.

spurs that frequently develop. Horses in pain throw their heads or shake them, bolt, buck, rear, or toss their heads violently as a result of pain in the mouth (remember fight or flight?). A painful problem in the mouth can also quickly radiate down the neck to the spine and even to the haunches.

The bridle and bit exert pressure on the head in five different sensitive areas beyond the mouth cavity. An ill-fitting bridle can rub the horse's cheekbones (an area that, like the bars of the mouth, has little cushion between the skin and bone, making it extremely sensitive). An ill-adjusted or fitted curb strap on a double or curb-type bridle can cause a horse pain in his chin groove. A too-small bit can rub the horse's lips and his cheeks. It also loses its effectiveness, because it is restricted into a straight-bar type of action. The center joint (in either a double or single-jointed bit) is no longer flexible.

If the horse is wearing a bit that doesn't fit, he doesn't understand what the rider is asking for. A too-large bit that slides side to side in the mouth can damage the tongue, the palate, and the lips. There is no stability in the mouth, and the connection with the rider is lost. It feels like a shoe that's too big. Such painful experiences cause the horse to dislike the bit and may lead to longer-term behavior problems or habits that are extremely difficult to break. For example, a horse ridden with a tight hand may try to cushion his bars against the bit by sticking his tongue out and slipping it between the bar and the bit's mouthpiece.

Understanding bitting takes a keen knowledge of the inside of your horse's mouth, and his particular anatomical attributes. An equine veterinarian who will let you look inside your horse's mouth and will explain your horse's unique structures is invaluable to the bitting process. You'll be able to determine the size of his mouth, the depth of his palate, the thickness of his tongue and the length of his bars. All are key to choosing the right bit.

CHAPTER 4

RIDING AND ANATOMY

To learn about horses' natural balance, watch as they caper in the pasture. When the horse is most animated and excited, his neck is highly arched and his head is almost perfectly perpendicular to the ground. He floats along with his tail up, his hooves light on the ground. When he's relaxed, walking from one patch of grass to the next, his neck is long and stretched out in front of him. His back muscles undulate gently and his walk is rhythmic and regular.

Other animals use their tails to help them balance. Horses have heads and necks to keep them in equilibrium. That's why the horse's head and neck move forward and up at the walk and canter at the same pace as their footfalls. When you add an unbalanced rider who interferes with the head and neck by pulling on the reins, or using the reins as a fulcrum from which to post the trot or stay in the saddle, he's disturbing the horse's central balancing system.

In *The Bit and the Reins*, Gerhard Kapitzke notes that the horse's back was not intended to carry the rider, nor was his mouth designed for bits. It just so happens that evolution and human ingenuity worked together to find a nice space on the horse to carry the saddle and a nice spot in the mouth for the bit. And so we have to be very aware of how we position ourselves in relation to the horse's anatomy.

To look at bitting from a holistic viewpoint, we take a horse's entire anatomy into consideration. Particularly important are the interrelationships between his mouth, neck, spine and surrounding muscles, and hindquarters. Because the hyoid bones are directly attached to both the tongue and the two large muscles of the neck, the flexing of the horse's poll, as well as the fulcrum action of the head and neck, are a kind of gateway to the bit's relationship with the body. Bitting problems often manifest in a stiff neck or a very tight topline. As the horse fights the bit, he stiffens his upper neck muscles—horses that travel "inverted" tend to develop muscles on the underside of their necks rather than over the top and along either side of their manes. They also might overdevelop the musculature on one side or the other.

Just as human beings suffer from "referred pain," where a shoulder injury, for example, could have an impact on hips, spine, and other muscles and bone structures that aren't local to the injury, so too do a horse's overall conditioning, how he is ridden, and how his bit and bridle fit refer sensations throughout the horse's body. Although we're always talking about "independent aids" in riding, don't confuse that with the way our body weight and balance—in short, everything we do with and to a horse—is interrelated and felt from head to tail.

Take a horse's locomotion, for example: As the horse moves forward, he pushes off the ground with his legs. The order of the hoof beats depends on the gait he's in. The action of the hind legs activates the large muscles of the hindquarters and the long muscles and ligaments of the back, followed by the ligaments and muscles in the neck. Those attach to the top of the head and the jaw. The elastic ligament in the neck is particularly important to horse locomotion

and bitting in that the *ligamentum nuchae* (or neck ligaments) extend from the thoracic vertebrae to the head and down the back. These ligaments allow the horse to support his head and neck without exerting muscle strength. As the horse moves, these ligaments adjust to the horse's head position to support it. The wide flat muscle under the neck ligaments and the *longissimus dorsi* along the spine are commonly referred to as the "topline" of the horse. These areas develop strength with proper training and allow the horse's back to swing gently as he moves under the rider and forward into the bit. They also develop to support the rider and the saddle. When a horse is wearing an ill-fitting saddle all the time, the muscles of his back will develop oddly.

The relationship between rider, equipment, and proper horse development holds true no matter the discipline. Watch the schooled cow horse as he stops, sits, and turns to move a cow; or the barrel horse as he pushes off from the starting gate; or even the trail horse as he pushes up a hill. Each and every horse, no matter what kind of tack, will move up and forward and over his back. It is the rider's responsibility to assure he's met with a soft hand and proper bit. In the desire to make our horses happy and healthy, assuring the use of a proper bit eliminates a host of problems.

33

A young horse uses his back muscles to propel forward.

CHAPTER - 5

THE ROLE OF THE RIDER

"The communication between the rider's hand and the horse's mouth must be completely without force, somewhat like a conversation between friends."
—Gerhard Kapitzke

If you imagine that this book is going to solve your training problems, you're wrong. As much as I'd like to provide all the answers, I'm only a writer and a researcher, not a sage, a telepathic, or an animal communicator.

36

If I've learned anything at all from the research conducted for this project, it's that every horse-and-rider combination faces a universe of options when it comes to bits and how the horse behaves in the bridle. Frequently, training problems that seem related to the horse's mouth have nothing at all to do with the bit. And you can only try so many bits before it becomes clear that the problem has more to do with you, or someone who trained him before you, or some other human-caused circumstance, than his bit.

You can spend a lot of money on bits—sweet iron, fat, skinny, jangly, jingly, with lozenge, without, rotated, not rotated—or you can abandon the bit search altogether and go back to basic training. This is the most important concept that I can put forward in this book. The bit is rarely the answer.

Consider this: The bit is a tool, like a screwdriver or a pitchfork, that can help us get the job done—it is one of many items in the equestrian's box of goodies, along with a saddle that fits, a properly adjusted bridle, a great veterinarian, and a farrier. Our other tools include our seat, legs, hands, and the way in which we apply and fit all of them together. Because the rider naturally upsets the horse's balance, the really important part of bitting is how the rider gives his signals to the horse and uses his tools. Just as there is a right way to hammer a nail into a plank, there's a correct way to apply each of our aids. And, since each horse is as highly individual as his rider, it's necessary to be both sensitive and adjustable.

If you don't have the right tools, each task becomes more onerous. Surely you can use the back of your shoe to hammer a nail into a board. But you might end up ruining the shoe or nursing a sore hand. A better way would be to find the perfect hammer with the perfect weight, to use the right size nail, and to get a carpenter to show you how to hammer correctly. The hammer you prefer may be quite different from the one your neighbor likes. Only you will know when you've found the one that works for you.

Most of us don't have any idea at all about how to find the proper bit. It's an experiment, the product of trial and error. Once a bit has been chosen, you may be happy with it for several months or years and then want to try something different. You may prefer one bit for riding at home and another for the trail; or it may take three bits to do the trick—one for home, one for the jumper ring, and one for horse shows. Just as a carpenter changes tools when a new task is presented to him, so must the equestrian consider what his horse is doing, where he's doing it, how the horse is likely to react to the situation, and the rider's awareness of how his horse is going to behave.

For example, a child on a pony may go perfectly in the arena at home, but bring

Every good craftsman has a big selection of tools. Having a variety of bits means you can experiment to see what suits you and your horse.

38

The bit is one part of the half-halt: a reminder to the horse to sit back on his haunches before a jump.

the pony to a horse show and suddenly he turns from steady Eddie to hot-to-trot. The child may not have mastered the aids, or the pony suddenly decides to ignore the child. Putting a stronger bit in the pony's mouth is an acceptable, although not ideal, solution. For safety's sake, slightly more mouth power is probably a good idea.

Event riders, as another example, frequently change from a snaffle bit to a leverage bit before heading off on the cross-country course. Leverage bits are illegal in the lower-level dressage portion of eventing, but many horses get hot on the cross-country course and riders need an extra element of "whoa" during this phase.

Some riders like to change bits more frequently; others ride in the same bit for years. It's a matter of personal preference and what works for your horse. There's no reason to change bits if everything is going well, meaning your horse travels obediently with his head, neck, and back relaxed. He listens to your seat and leg aids, and is working correctly. As the old adage goes, "If it ain't broke, don't fix it."

A horse's intended discipline will also have an impact on his training and bitting—whether dressage, jumper, reiner, working cow horse, or regular ol' Joe backyard horse. In each discipline, the philosophy of bitting (but not the same general purpose) varies. For example, during the research phase of writing this book, I read two articles, back to back. The first, written by 1984 Olympic dressage medalist Hilda Gurney, detailed the use of popular bit styles: The loose ring, the eggbutt, and the full cheek. "The full cheek

is legal in dressage but rarely used—it is assumed our horses can turn," Gurney wrote. Subsequently I read an article by Jeff Cook, a renowned hunter/jumper trainer, who actually recommended the full cheek snaffle to help the horse turn. Indeed, it is assumed that all horses in both the dressage and hunter worlds can turn, but why would these disciplines, both of which appear based on submissive, forward horses, have such a different attitude toward the same piece of hardware? The answer may lie in the fact that, in the hunter ring, horses are expected to travel with their noses slightly out, with a less rounded, upright frame and not as much flexion in the jaw. They are often asked to turn with outside aids. The dressage horse's turns are smoothly bent around the rider's inside leg. While all horses need lateral flexibility in the mouth, jaw, poll, neck, and body to work correctly—which is easier to achieve with a loose ring bit than with a fixed ring version—equestrian disciplines emphasize different elements due to the nature of the skills needed during the activity.

Interestingly, the equestrian disciplines are still somewhat snobbish about their training methods, despite the fact that we're all born of the same Asian and European techniques. Few dressage riders would accept the training methods of a hunter rider, and the opposite is also true. Luckily for our horses, this is changing, albeit slowly. Some dressage shows now offer Western classes and jumper trainers are signing up for dressage lessons.

Nonetheless, what's acceptable in casual training (not including what's written in the

40

A horse in piaffe demonstrates the use of the hindquarters. Notice how slack the curb rein is.

official rule books) in one discipline may be totally disparaged by another. Western riders regularly use what dressage gurus would consider a severe, high-ported curb bit with long shanks. Such split-second precision to remind the horse to flex at the poll serves nearly the same purpose as the double bridle in high-level dressage. Both disciplines have the same training goal: the very lightest, fleetest horse ridden with great finesse.

percent of the time. The activity and leverage of the bit is rarely needed. The weight of romal reins is enough to remind the horse of the rider's contact.

Pressure on the reins reminds the horse to balance or to flex, sending a message to the horse to pay attention, to rebalance, or to listen to the rider's seat. The Western pleasure rider wants it all to look effortless—a lightly held hand, smooth gaits, motionless rider, all to be executed unnoticed by the judge. The dressage rider, too, seeks subtleness in his control, embodying harmony and oneness with the horse. The jumper rider, on the other hand, needs the ability to sit his horse back on his haunches, quickly rebalance, turn, and gallop forward, all measured in tenths of a second. The ultimate aim—balance, a horse whose head, neck, back, and haunches are working correctly to propel him forward—is the same.

Whatever your discipline, however, every bit has the potential to be a harsh bit in the wrong hands. Take the high-ported Western bits as an example: as the rider lifts his hand slightly, sits back in the saddle, and uses his voice, the well-trained horse will know that the rider wants him to slow down. That attuned rider will immediately release any pressure as a reward to the horse.

Now, imagine the rider isn't so refined. Instead of the instant release to the horse's response, he continues to pull. The bit starts to press on the horse's bars, the curb strap presses on the chin groove and the port, depending on its height, makes contact with the roof of the mouth. The horse may slow down, but since there's no reward (the

The spade bit is another example—the uneducated eye may see it as a horrific instrument of torture. But the reality is quite different. The well-trained Western bridle horse rarely needs the influence of the hand to do his job. When he is properly ridden, the bit sits comfortably against his tongue 99.9

41

release) he doesn't know what the rider wants and keeps pushing against the bit. Then the rider, in frustration, gives the horse a big, hard jerk in the mouth. This may stop the horse, but it may also make him defensive. His head will go in the air, he'll open his mouth, and he may even start to rear. Same bit. Two entirely different responses.

Every discipline shares a basic training scale. Think of it as a pyramid—with the levels building upon each other. The levels are:

- Rhythm
- Relaxation and suppleness
- Readiness or contact
- Engagement and impulsion
- Straightness

No matter what kind of tack you ride in, one of the first steps of horse training is to ask the horse to maintain a nice steady gait ("rhythm"). Early on, trainers do this on the longe line or in the round pen. Once you've added a rider and a bridle (a soft snaffle bit is the first a horse should wear) and saddle, the horse is asked to maintain that rhythm, learning to balance with the rider on his back while staying relaxed and supple. Note that "readiness" or "contact"—where the horse willingly accepts the rider and his aids—is fairly high on the pyramid. This is the point at which a Western rider may switch to a curb bit (the horse has already developed a soft mouth and an understanding of flexion of the jaw and poll).

Proper training—in that the horse has accepted the aids—is crucial to a horse's

success and will make bitting a fairly simple exercise. A well-trained and happy horse may wear the same bit his entire life. But when those basics are lacking, it may be best to return to step one and teach the horse to trust the aids. All of this is vitally important to figuring out which bit is best. Riders should assess a checklist of other possibilities, including that it's the rider himself that's causing the problem. In fact, nine times out of ten, the root of a problem is the human rather than the horse or the equipment.

For a clear example of how bad riding has an impact on a horse, watch some beginner lessons. Beginners are sometimes taught that the bit "controls" the horse. In fact, many riding schools still teach "kick to go, pull to stop" methods, when in fact there are a dozen different small signals in each communication with the horse. The kick-and-pull method is simplistic and misleading. The bit and the reins are a communication device—a guide to the horse, rather than a steering wheel.

Note how difficult it is for beginners to post to the trot without their hands following their bodies—up and down, up and down. It gets even worse when beginners start to learn to sit the trot. Without a strong core, proper alignment with the rider's body centered over the horse's center, or the ability to keep their hands still, riders bounce hard on the horse's back, trying to maintain balance using their hands. The horse feels it through the bit—bang, bang, bang—against the bars of his mouth and his lips. His back and neck tighten in defensiveness, and it becomes even more difficult for the rider to remain balanced. The main reason school horses tend to be "hard mouthed" is that they've had a million beginners bouncing away on their mouths and backs. Their necks are stiff, they have no soft flexion in their jaws, and they harden up in defensiveness.

The beginner rider—or any rider, for that matter—needs to learn to control the horse with subtle hands. That "elastic" or soft contact good riders seek comes when the rider no longer needs either stirrups or reins to balance.

Even experienced riders have bad habits that cause the horse to stiffen and tighten his jaw. Some riders position themselves behind the vertical, centered position and while they may look like they have quiet hands, in fact they may be "waterskiing" on the horse's mouth. Others may have such soft, nonexistent contact with the bit that it serves no purpose at all. There are riders who have no idea that the timing of contact with the bit is directly related to the timing of the gaits or the movement you'd like to execute. Finally there are the riders that still think "steering" means pulling the reins left or right, as if the reins were the wheels of an automobile. There are many different kinds of rein direction—flexion, direct, indirect, neck reining, different placement of the hand for neck reining, and so forth. Riding a horse well requires a very large vocabulary of signals, as well as the ability to read a horse's responses and apply the right aid at the right time. It is a highly complex exercise and one at the center of the horse riding craft we love so well. The bit is a small piece of the whole.

The ideal, whether you're riding English, Western, or bareback, is a conversational contact. The horse should know you're there through the reins, but he shouldn't in any way feel as if you're pulling (unless he's in a full-blown, running-away-with-you panic, in which case you'll need more than the bit—you'll need an emergency stop). The bit works together with the other signals you give your horse. If you want him to collect up, add leg and close your hand. If you want him to bend, use inside leg and ask him with the rein to flex his jaw. The rider should know to use the other aids—seat and legs— before applying rein pressure.

The misuse of the bit, related to an unsteady rider seat and miscued and misunderstood aids, has a domino effect on the horse's body. A rider who bounces against the horse's mouth because of an unsteady contact causes the following:

1) The horse gets confusing messages: Go forward? Stop? Go slow? He has no way of telling what the rider wants because horses don't understand intentions—they only understand clear messages.

2) The horse may feel pain. Given that he's tuned for either fight or flight he'll likely react with one of those two reactions. He'll either try to run from the pressure, or he'll get into fight mode, tensing his back and perhaps tossing his head or even "rooting" against the bit.

43

In chapter 3, we discussed how the horse's head and neck operate as a fulcrum-balancing device, his poll connecting all the muscles down his topline. With such confusing messages from the rider, the horse will inevitably tighten his back, which makes it even that much harder for the rider to balance. A horse that is soft, supple, and swinging through his topline is much easier to ride than one with his head in the air and

44

Resistance to the bit can be quite obvious. Here, the horse is protesting the rider's too-heavy hands.

his back muscles rigid. The more rigid and tight the back is, the harder the gaits. The harder the gaits, the more difficult it is for the rider to be comfortably seated. The rigid back can also create soreness in the horse's

sacroiliac, withers, and neck. All of that can radiate down the legs and make the horse appear off or even lame.

A rider who takes a death grip on the reins can easily cause what's called "rein lameness," where the rein contact is actually inhibiting the horse's balance, causing his back to tighten up and stopping the steady rhythm of the gait. At the walk, rein lameness is likely to manifest as a "lateral" walk, where the horse isn't stepping forward in a one-two-three-four rhythm but rather a "one-two, one-two" rhythm. Any working horse should have a clearly defined rhythm at any gait, and following, soft hands will assure that. A busy, inflexible death grip or ill-timed rein aids will cause rhythm and balance problems.

In the scale of training, contact appears after rhythm and suppleness. The horse and the rider have to be able to work comfortably in a rhythm and the horse needs a soft and supple way of going before contact can be established with the bit. If the horse is tense or tight, he won't accept the contact, no matter what discipline you practice.

How do bits and the reins work together? The rein and the seat regulate forward motion, determine direction and flexion, and can, on occasion, be used as an emergency brake for an unresponsive horse. However, a well-trained horse needs very little in the way of rein aids. Consider natural horsemanship trainers who have built strong relationships with their equines. They're able to ride without bridles. The well-schooled dressage rider can bring a horse from an extended

45

46

canter to a collected canter with only the use of his seat and a slight touch of the rein.

Most of us will never ride at that level and need only to know that our horses will walk, trot, canter, turn, and maybe jump a few little obstacles or navigate a trail. Most of us do not need such finesse. Nonetheless, there's a lesson to be learned from such expertise: The upper-level reiner rides his pattern with slack reins—the less he does with his hand, the higher his score. Watch him maneuver his body: it's a highly tuned communication tool that gives subtle signals. The dressage rider keeps a steady, soft contact, the hunter rider navigates jumps with a light hand, each discipline with a different way of carrying the reins and the contact with the bit, but ultimately striving for the same goal—a conversation with the horse's mouth, head, neck, and topline that originates mostly from the other aids—the seat and the leg—and not from the hand.

So why bother with bits at all? Indeed, there is a movement afoot to dispense with them, as some horses don't like metal or bits in general and some riders, trainers, and scientists believe they are cruel, and that we've been trapped by tradition. After all, bits do operate on the principle that a little "pressure" (i.e., pain) can control the horse. Of course, the hackamore has been around for centuries, but there are a few new options. "Bitless bridles" have been developed by Dr. Robert Cook, a professor at Tufts University, and Monica Lehmenkühler, a horse trainer and rider based in Cologne,

Photo by: Dusty Perin

The bitless hackamore uses leverage, initiated from the rein. It applies pressure to the poll and the bridge of the nose.

Germany, that each use different pressure points on the head to communicate with the horse (see chapter 10).

◀ With a soft mouth and an engaged topline, Matt Mills and his horse are the picture of harmony.

Despite their seeming gentleness, a bitless bridle can still be severe. Indeed, some mechanical hackamores can be harsher than a bitted bridle, and in the wrong hands can do some serious damage to the horse's nose cartilage—a sensitive and relatively soft structure. Bitted bridles use some of the same pressure—for example, when a rider pulls back on the reins, the horse feels the pressure on the cheek and the poll. Different rein positions have different effects on both the bitted and the bitless horse, with lower hands having a more direct pull on the bars or the lower part of the nose, while higher hands have an impact on the lips or the cheeks in the bitless version.

Unless we're well schooled in natural horsemanship and have highly trained horses, most of us still need a bit or a bitless bridle. Even so, we should strive to train ourselves and our horses to go with the lightest, most subtle contact possible. Instead of focusing on choosing the correct bit, choose the right training for yourself and for the horse.

Every horse, no matter the discipline, can be easily started in a regular old snaffle bit. The horse should be taught by a competent trainer to walk, trot, and canter from seat and leg cues, understanding through the voice, reinforced with the seat, and finally, only after the horse has blown off the other aids, through a quick "pressure and release" with the bit. Later, as the horse becomes more trained and is able to stop, go, and steer effectively and without resistance, the rider can consider moving to a different bit. In a lot of cases, the horse can stay in the snaffle forever. The Western rider might want to put a shanked bit on his horse, and if that's the case, he'll need to introduce it properly after the horse is responsive in the snaffle and understands neck reining.

Learn to ride with your seat and legs.

CHAPTER 6

THE GREAT UNIVERSE OF BITS

"You cannot buy your way out of a training problem."
—Julie Goodnight

One of the ambiguities of the bitting world that will remain as long as there is a free market, innovative bit makers, and demand by riders, is whether we really *need* all these bits or whether they are the invention of marketers looking to sell us the latest and greatest invention. Bit makers sell the illusion to some people that riding will be easier with a new bit and all problems will be solved.

Looking closely at the world's collections of ancient bits, it's easy to see that little has changed over the past thousands of years. The ancient curb is very much like the modern curb; the snaffle is still a snaffle.

Surely some of the new developments in bits have been a godsend for our horses. Metallurgy, for example, has come a long way since the Bronze Age, and we're now able to produce bits that suit our particular horses' taste buds, or that wear more evenly, or that produce a softer mouth. We know from science that certain metals stimulate our horses' sense of taste. Certain polymers work well for those horses that don't like metal in their mouths, and we even have apple-flavored bits, although whether these are manufactured for horses or for their human owners is an unanswerable question. That's good news for horses and riders because no matter how finicky your horse, there's always the possibility that you can find a bit that works. And if you can't, there are custom bit makers, such as Jay Shuttleworth, who makes custom bits for high-level hunter/jumper riders on the East Coast; Greg Darnall, one of the foremost Western bitting experts; and Wilson Capron, whose stunning artwork and fine craftsmanship are unmatched.

Why would you need a custom bit when there are so many options on the market?

Perhaps there's something special you'd like represented on your shanks (if you're a Western rider) for your show horse in the Western pleasure ring. Another reason to seek out a custom bit maker is that your horse has a unique mouth. Perhaps he has a jaw that's not quite straight or a very low palate.

Custom bit makers are capable of recreating antique bits, modifying current styles, altering shapes and widths, adding a ring in the center of a lozenge, and about anything you might want. But be warned that a poorly made bit can have disastrous results: a sharp piece or malformed angle can injure your horse's mouth and make him reluctant to "take" the bit at all, so make sure your custom bit maker is reputable and skilled.

A hunter must stretch over his neck and topline.

There are so many bit choices available now that it's worth borrowing bits from friends to get an idea as to whether your horse goes better in a different kind of bit, rather than spending a lot of money on either buying bits or having one made. But if you should find that your horse has a special quirk, an odd-shaped mouth, or some other unique problem, seeking out a custom loriner is a great option.

Despite the lack of significant changes in bits since they were invented, there have been some notable innovations, borne out of our understanding of equine anatomy, that have made them more comfortable. For example, angling the mouthpiece, or a portion of it, at 45 degrees can make it lie more comfortably on the horse's tongue. The mouthpiece may also be elevated so it more naturally follows the arc of the horse's tongue. There are other new shapes and many more sizes, acknowledging the wide variation in horse mouths.

Mass customization—the mass production of goods with differing individual specifications through the use of components that may be assembled in a number of different configurations—has been fully embraced by bit makers since the seventeenth century. It's an important concept in bitting because it allows the rider to choose a single style of mouthpiece— say, medium thin single-jointed—and then decide what kinds of cheeks would help the horse perform best. As you read through the upcoming chapters, remember that these days, just about any of the standard mouthpieces come with any of the standard cheeks, and vice-versa. Nearly every bit is available with a variety of mouthpieces or different materials. Some bits even come with adjustable mouthpieces, which means you can own one bit and change the size for several horses.

Those early loriners of the sixteenth and seventeenth centuries acknowledged the bit as a whole rather than simply a mouthpiece and cheek piece. In other words, for a bit to be most effective, every aspect of it has to be considered at once. Some bits today actually allow you to customize them without buying a completely new bit. Mikmar combination bits, for example, have a high port, a copper roller in the center, and a thin rope across the nose. They have become favorites of some top jumper riders for their adjustability. You can move the reins into various positions on the shanks and the noseband so it is possible to change the leverage on the bit, the poll, and the nose pressure to uniquely suit your horse. It allows the rider to customize the bit's pressure points without changing the bit's mouthpiece.

Another company that developed its own style and family of bits is Myler. Their products have a signature curved mouthpiece that keeps the pressure off the tongue. They also sell different kinds of mouthpieces with the same general shape, such as a curb with an arch-shaped mouthpiece. Many of their bits have a barrel roller in the middle that encourages the horse to play with the bit and keep a softer mouth.

Thanks to University of Michigan bitting studies, in which radiography examined the position of five different kinds of bits in the horse's mouth, we now know much more about what happens as different types of rein pressure are applied. The study, performed by J. Manfredi, Hilary Clayton, and D. Rosenstein, noted the differences in bit position with rein contact and without rein contact. The scientists also noted the distance of each of the bits from the premolars with rein tension and without rein tension. They discovered that certain bits did change position in the horse's mouth when rein pressure was applied, while other bits did not. That seems to verify that some horses are more comfortable in certain types of bits due to the shapes of their mouths. Therefore, it is in the horse's best interest that our trainers, marketers, and product developers keep working to make the horse comfortable.

Of course, the more options we have for our horses, the better off we all are. The only way the carpenter knows, for example, that one hammer works better than another is by trying them out. Such is the case with the bit—trial and error, combined with some knowledge of theory, is the best method.

Some horse trainers have many bits for just that reason. Depending on the horse, the rider, and the situation, the trainer may try some different options. Several trainers told me during the course of my research that simply getting rid of a harsh bit and using a mild one made them look like heroes because the horse relaxed almost instantly. Sometimes the problem was the horse had been ridden with a completely different kind of contact and bit before it came to the trainer. Experimenting was the only way to figure out what the horse was most comfortable with.

Even the most impeccably trained horse occasionally needs a change to "freshen" him up. That doesn't necessarily mean you need to put in a double-twisted wire after riding in a plain snaffle. It might mean swapping out a full cheek for a loose ring, or a French link for a KK Ultra. You may try the same curb bit in sweet iron, which is more porous than steel, rusts more easily, and lacks steel's bitter taste. But you have to give it time. Changing bits will undoubtedly produce a response the very first day you ride with your new bit. The question is, what kind of response will it produce on day three, four, or five? What about day ten, day ninety, or year four?

Once the horse has habituated to the "newness" of it, you'll be able to see whether he's responding differently to the bridle. The differences can be subtle, so the rider needs to be sensitive and knowledgeable about the horse's way of going. It may only be after a few weeks that the rider will feel the difference in his horse after changing out a bit, especially if it's a subtle change. Perhaps the horse has been too fussy in his mouth, and the rider is seeking the same softness but without the busy jaw. Perhaps the rider wants slightly more response to his half-halt, or to reinforce the "sit" in a reining horse. In this case, he might switch to a quicker bit. We'll discuss more about which bits produce what kinds of results later in the chapters on the specific families of bits.

53

In some rare cases, you may come across a horse that's had such bad riding and training that he's learned to lean on the bit, balancing on it as if it were almost a fifth leg. No amount of jiggling or moving the bit creates any response. With such a case, you might find that changing bits is going to have little impact on the horse—he'll continue to lean and ignore that bit no matter what you put in his mouth. The horse has not engaged his hindquarters, or perhaps has an ill-fitting saddle, or has been ridden by a rider who hangs on the contact without release.

An early fix would have been to school more effective response to the seat and legs, whereby the rider changes her position and rocks the horse back onto his haunches, which allows him to lighten his front end and soften his mouth. The rider that applies steady, unending pressure without release and without the direction of the seat created the problem. The same holds true for horses that run through the bit.

It's also possible that a horse experiencing physical pain in his hind end—either his haunches, his stifles, or his hocks—may have difficulty sitting back and lifting his

front end. By traveling on the forehand, he's attempting to relieve the pain in his hind end. In this case, the rider would do well to have the horse examined by a vet, especially if the heaviness in the bit is a relatively new development, all other things being equal.

Besides physical pain in the back or hindquarters, a change in rider can be another cause for discomfort. A bit that works wonderfully in one rider's hands may be a disaster in another's. Greg Darnall, renowned Western bitting expert, notes in the *Western Horseman* article "A Bit on Bits:" "Suppose a trainer shows a reining horse in a bit that has some leverage to it and a quick pull. He gets along just fine with the horse because he has good hands. But if a heavy handed amateur rider were to show the horse in the same bit and pulls too quick or too hard, he will not get the nice, fluid stop the trainer did."

All aids, whether the seat, the legs, or the hands, should be used in such a way that there's a moment of pressure followed by a quick moment of release. It is only in this way that a rider develops a light response in his partner. The pressure is minute, lightning fast, and should produce a reaction. In that way, the horse and the rider are having a conversation about what the rider wants. "Forward, now." "Balance, now." "Lateral, now, now, now." A steady leg pressure deadens the horse to the aids just as a steady rein pressure deadens his responsive mouth. When an unrelenting hardness is applied to the bit, the horse becomes deaf to the rein aid. It's like the boy who cried wolf—a constant pressure that signals nothing. Then,

when the rider actually needs the horse to respond, he no longer has the tool at his disposal.

A horse with such resistance to the bit probably won't salivate or chew very much, if at all. A well-trained, happy horse should go along with a wet mouth. It doesn't have to be dripping, but he should exhibit at least a little moisture. This is both a sign that the horse hears your signals and that he's comfortable. It would be nearly impossible for a horse with a locked jaw to have a wet mouth, since saliva is produce by relaxed chewing. A wet mouth shows the horse's mouth is free and light. A locked mouth is dry and has the sensation of being "hard" and inflexible, both to the touch and to the bit.

When working with a young horse, it's a great idea to mess around with his mouth—run your fingers along the bars, play with the tongue, gently slide your forefingers over the area of the horse's mouth where the bit will eventually go. This will habituate the horse to the feeling of the bit and also make him less defensive to having foreign objects, whether a veterinarian's hand, paste wormer, or a bit, in his mouth.

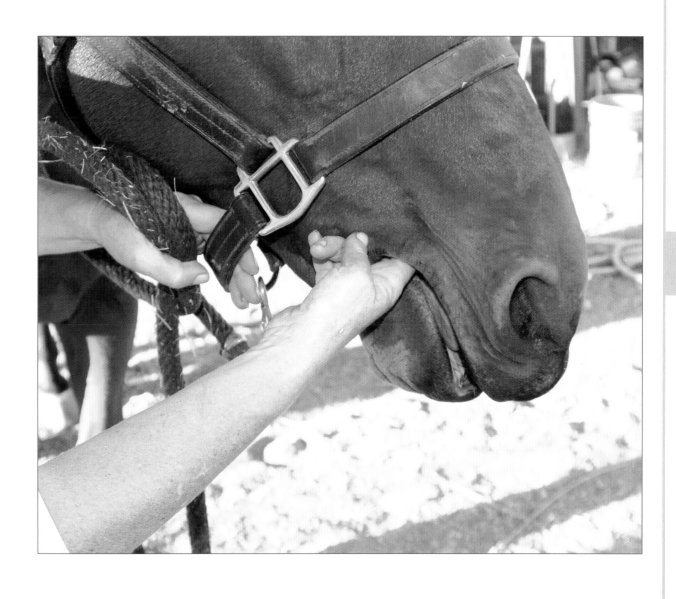

CHAPTER - 7

WHAT BITS ARE MADE OF

Horses have taste preferences. Experimenting with various materials may reveal that a horse prefers sweet iron over stainless steel, or a polyurethane product such as Nathe (a type of plastic manufactured in Germany and used in bits).

All metals are combinations of elements. The "recipe" for each metal listed below determines its taste, its durability, and whether or not it will easily oxidize when in contact with saliva. The metals are a bit like skin: some have many open pores and some don't. The pores determine how easily the bit rusts. The more porous the metal, the more likely it is to rust, and unlike your old plumbing or the body of your automobile, rust is a good thing in horse bits. It sweetens the taste of the metal.

These days, many bits are made from combinations of different metals. They may have a stainless steel mouthpiece with a copper roller in the center, for example, or a copper mouthpiece with stainless rings for durability. Also, several manufacturers are making steel bits with copper inlays,

both for texture and for taste. Bits also can be made of other materials such as rubber or plastic, sometimes in combination with metals.

Some horses may prefer the taste of steel to copper, or vulcanite to Nathe. It is worth trying a variety of materials in your horse's mouth to see which one he likes best. Also, you might find that his taste changes over time. A young horse might like a big fat rubber bit, but as he becomes more acclimated to having something in his mouth and becomes more responsive to the aids, a stainless steel bit may suit him better. Try plenty of different bits to find the "key" that unlocks your horse's best self.

STAINLESS STEEL

Stainless steel is the most popular bit material used today. It tends to be light and durable, although the quality largely depends on where it is manufactured. Some bit companies have moved their factories to Asia, where the quality of the steel may be less than ideal and the manufacturing process sometimes careless. If you purchase a stainless steel bit, especially an inexpensive one, keep an eye on it to make sure it retains its integrity and does not have any burrs or deformities.

The best stainless steel bits are made in Europe using the lost wax casting method, which is nearly as old as the horse bit itself. The method uses a wax cast to create the shape of the object. Molten steel is poured into the mold and then solidified into the desired shape. The process ensures the metal pieces are smooth.

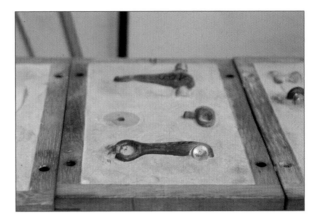

Bit makers still use the "lost wax" casting method. They make a mold of the bit's shape and then pour molten metal alloy into the mold to harden into the bit's individual pieces.

Quality stainless steel bits do not pit, wear evenly, and are very long lasting. While some horses like stainless steel, it tends not to have much impact on whether a horse salivates or not—it has a neutral taste and smell.

COPPER

One of the softest metals around, copper is a great option for horse bits because of its taste. While it can wear faster and more unevenly than stainless steel, a lot of horses very much like it. The sweetish taste of copper encourages the horse to salivate, so try one if your horse is routinely dry-mouthed for no obvious reason. There are very few pure copper bits on the market today because they don't hold up well,

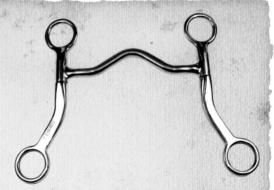

The copper on this bit promotes salivation. Most copper bits have steel cheeks for durability.

but there are plenty of bits with copper components, such as rollers, balls, barrels, or mouthpieces. The rings tend to be made of stainless steel for durability. It's worth noting that a copper bit alone won't cause a horse to accept the bit—it may help him like the taste better, and salivate more because of the process of oxidation, but bit acceptance can be a training issue, not always a bit issue.

SWEET IRON

Sweet iron isn't actually iron at all, but steel. The process of bitmaking with sweet iron, also called cold-rolled steel, is somewhat different from stainless. Contrary to the lost-wax process of bitmaking, cold-rolled steel is cooled and then shaped, rather than cast in a mold while hot. It's dense, but also much softer than stainless and more prone to rust. Some horses like the flavor of sweet iron as much as they like copper, or even more. The taste of sweet iron encourages salivation. Many Western bits use this material, and lately more English bit makers have started using it as well. It is durable and a good bitting material.

The Trust Bit series is made of sweet iron. Generally, sweet iron bits are dark blue or black.

60

ALUMINUM

Likely the least expensive and lightest bitting material made today, aluminum is not really recommended. The metal has a bitter taste and a drying effect on the horse's mouth. Aluminum bits have largely gone out of fashion.

ALUMINUM BRONZE

Don't confuse aluminum and aluminum bronze, however. Aluminum bronze is 90 percent copper, 10 percent aluminum combination that is bronze in color because of its high copper content. It has the taste of copper but the durability of aluminum.

GERMAN SILVER

Contrary to the name, German silver is actually an alloy of different metals. The usual formulation is 60 percent copper, 20 percent nickel, and 20 percent zinc, but in horse bits the nickel and zinc components may comprise slightly more or less than in that formula. German silver bits taste sweeter than regular stainless steel, but are not as sweet or tasty as pure copper. They are generally expensive (depending on the country of origin of the manufacturer) but do encourage salivation in some horses. German silver bits are not as shiny as regular bright stainless, and tend to need more vigorous cleaning.

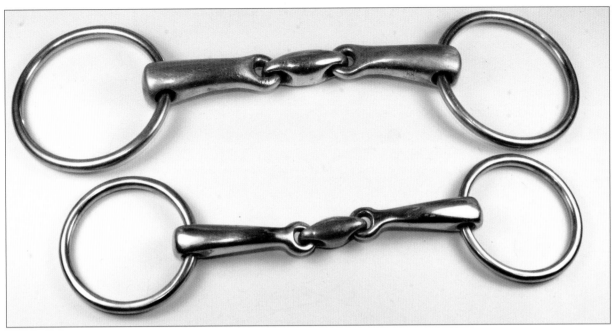

Compare this German silver bit, top, with the combination steel and copper bit below it. You can see the subtle gold color of the German silver.

AURIGAN

Another alloy, Aurigan (pronounced "oregone") is made up of 85 percent copper, 4 percent silicon, and 11 percent zinc. Note that Aurigan lacks nickel as a component. Some horses, just as some people, are quite allergic to nickel, so Aurigan is a good choice for a horse that reacts to bits made with nickel. Aurigan's high copper content means it has the advantage of copper's sweet taste and oxidation, while being much stronger than pure copper. Aurigan was invented by scientists working with Herm Sprenger. The company holds the patent on the material, so Sprenger makes all Aurigan bits.

Sprenger created a new alloy called Aurigan that contains a large amount of copper. It has copper's "sweetness," but is more durable.

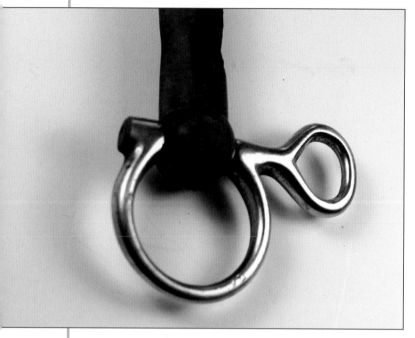

A rubber Baucher that's showing a fair amount of wear.

RUBBER

Soft, flexible, and relatively neutral from a taste standpoint, rubber's biggest drawback is its tendency to pit and wear unevenly. Almost all rubber bits have some kind of metal core to give them more stability in the mouth. Sometimes it's a wire, sometimes a bar. A horse's teeth can easily cause damage to the bit, so daily inspection is vital. Horses with mouths that are very sensitive to metal tend to like bits made of alternative materials such as rubber, vulcanite, Nathe, or polyurethane (see below). Rubber is the least durable of these alternative materials.

VULCANITE

In bitting, vulcanite is the answer to rubber's durability problem. A hard rubber, vulcanite was invented in 1840s. A vulcanite (as well as rubber) mouthpiece tends to be very thick and thus very soft for horses that have enough space in their mouths. You can often find vulcanite-covered bits, such as a metal single-jointed snaffle covered with vulcanite.

Vulcanite, rubber, and Happy Mouth bits can come with metal cores or without.

NATHE

Another German invention, Nathe is a synthetic material similar in properties to straight plastic—it's stiff but still somewhat flexible, and you generally don't need a metal core like you would for a rubber bit. Note that Nathe, just like all synthetics or non-metal bits, has a much shorter lifespan. Horses will chew through them. It is a much thinner option for horses that like rubber or vulcanite but can't handle the bulk in their mouths.

LEATHER

Relatively rare for no real reason, leather bits are nearly impossible to find in the U.S. but are still on tack store shelves in Europe. Leather bits have a number of advantages, particularly for highly sensitive horses who dislike all the above materials. Leather bits need to be cared for extremely carefully, because saliva can erode them quickly. They do, however, work well for very sensitive-mouthed horses since they are flexible and gentle on the mouth.

Some horses prefer heavier bits, some prefer lighter bits, and some prefer something in between. To get to know the different materials bits are made from, visit your local tack store and test the different weights and finishes of a variety of bits. The Aurigan or German silver bits will likely be the heaviest, followed by the stainless steel

HAPPY MOUTH

Another brand name that's sometimes imitated, Happy Mouth bits are made of engineered plastic, and they usually have an apple flavoring. Happy Mouths have a distinctive "ripple" texture that encourages the horse to chew the bit. Happy Mouths are another alternative to thick rubber or vulcanite bits.

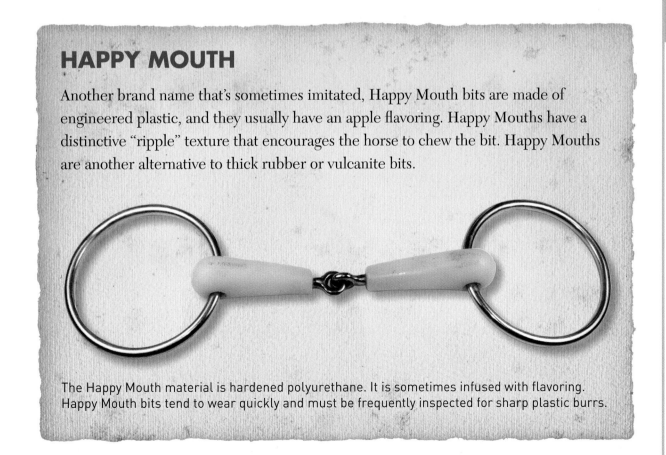

The Happy Mouth material is hardened polyurethane. It is sometimes infused with flavoring. Happy Mouth bits tend to wear quickly and must be frequently inspected for sharp plastic burrs.

bits. The shape of the bits will also have an impact on weight. Some horses like a very light bit, and in this case you might consider a hollow mouthpiece. Others prefer a heft around which they can close their mouths. It really comes down to equine preference.

Although we mentioned salivation in our roundup of bit materials, a horse can be salivating and still not accepting the bit. A horse's anatomy is programmed to salivate when he chews or when a foreign object enters his mouth. Jessica Jahiel points out in her book on bits that the "context of the salivation" is key to determining whether the horse is truly happy in his bit. Sensitive horsemen learn to observe the whole horse, from head to toe, to determine whether he's content. Is the horse's neck tight? Are his under-neck muscles tense? Is his back stiff? Are his ears pinned or perked? Are his

nostrils wrinkled? Is his tail swishing irritably? All of these actions signal discomfort. A horse could be salivating and yet still be unhappy about his bitting situation.

It's been proven by one German university that the material out of which a bit is fashioned does have an impact on a horse's salivation. Ideally, though, if a horse is comfortable and happy in his bit, the material *encourages* salivation rather than creates it. On the other hand, a non-salivating horse may be perfectly happy in his bit. There is simply no black and white answer.

Be wary of gimmicks or bits that promise to manufacture an effect that only a happy, well-trained horse and rider combination can actually achieve. The house is only as solid as the nails driven into the stud, and those are only as good the carpenter's skill with his hammer.

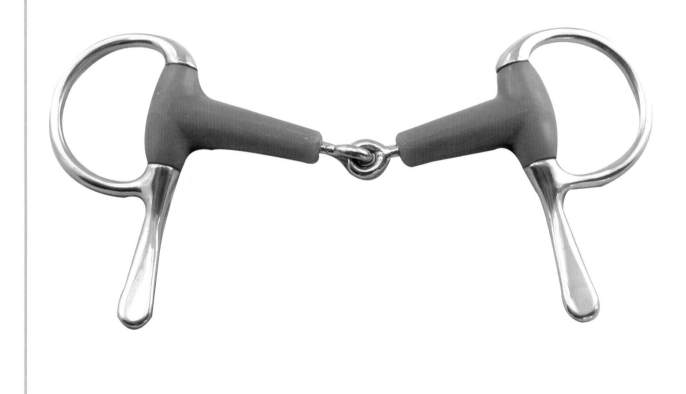

CHAPTER - 8

MANUFACTURE, SELECTION, AND CARE OF BITS

Why are some bits so expensive? For one thing, the raw materials out of which quality bits are fashioned are relatively expensive to produce. The second reason is that a well-made bit must touch many human hands before it is complete. That means a high cost of labor.

Yes, some bits are made in automated factories. You can usually tell these bits from the handmade kind because they might have some rough edges or welds, they might feel unbalanced, they might have uneven coloring, or their links and connections may not be smooth.

CUSTOM BITS

If you were to hire one of the custom bit makers, here's what would happen: The bit maker would come to your horse. First he would talk with you about what particular problem you were trying to solve, or what you were looking for in a bit. Then he'd likely take a good look at and, most importantly, feel of the horse's mouth by sticking his index and second fingers inside to gauge the width of the bars, the thickness of the tongue, and the height of the palate. He'd roll back the horse's lips to see how his teeth align and the shape of his bite. A skilled bit maker would want to see you ride your horse. He would note the subtleties of the horse's movement, areas of tension, and how the horse was reacting to rein pressure and other rider aids. He'd question you about what you'd hope to accomplish with a new bit. Once he had determined those specifics, he would go off to his workshop—a metal working shop—and begin to fashion your bit.

HIGH-QUALITY MASS-PRODUCED BITS

On a bigger scale, the Herm Sprenger factory in Germany has been making high-end English bits for over one hundred years. While the company turns out lots of bits, each one is still crafted by a human being. The process begins with a mold of wax in the shape of each particular bit's mouthpiece. In the case of the single-jointed snaffle, for example, the mold is in the shape of the canons (mouthpieces)—the two pieces will be welded together after all the parts are made. Then hot metal is poured into the mold and allowed to harden (See page 59).

Next, the piece moves to the assembly stage. Holes are made in either end for the insertion of the rings and the joint is fixed to the center of the bit. At this stage, the decision is made as to what kind of cheek or ring the bit will have—D, full cheek, eggbutt, and so on. Then the bit is smoothed in a vat of stones and hand-polished, packed, and shipped to your local tack store or your doorstep. Even though the process for making bits may be more automated than it was in past centuries, the basic theory remains unchanged.

68

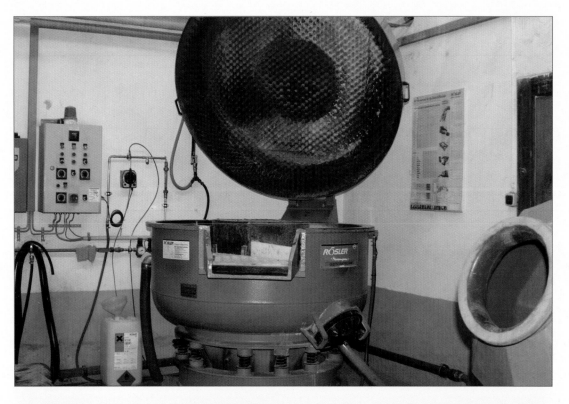

After the casting process, bit pieces are assembled. The rings are attached to the canons.
The bit is then hand- and machine-polished. The vat in this photo contains smooth stones for
that purpose.

ASSESSING BIT QUALITY

It is important to know the bit-making process to understand quality. When you consider buying a bit, make sure you feel it carefully. Run your hands over the edges: the bit should be smooth and no burrs should catch on your skin. Pay particular attention to the connection points where the bit has been welded together by either man or machine. The joints should be smooth. The skin around the horse's mouth, and particularly the corners of the lips, is thin and sensitive. A poorly made bit that pinches or pokes could cause the horse to begin to resist the bit, toss his head, and become irritated with the bridle in general.

While there are many well-made bits in the world, there are also plenty of poorly made bits. The quality of the raw material is important (see chapter 7), as is the fabrication process. Machine-made bits may be less expensive, but they won't have been subjected to the scrutiny of an individual, and thus could have defects. You can buy a perfectly good bit for less than $100; just know that the bit needs to meet your quality requirements or you could create an inadvertent horse-training problem.

Another inspection bit buyers need to undertake is the balance test. With a jointed bit, drape it across the back of your hand or your forearm. The center joint should be in the center of your arm or hand. Let it rest there. Does it feel as if you have equal weight on either side of your hand? Because bits are made in pieces, it is quite possible that one side could be slightly heavier than the other. A well-constructed bit should feel precisely balanced on either side.

69

Test your bit's balance by laying it across either your fingers or the back of your hand. Does it feel even? Are the rings the same size and the same angle? This bit is actually slightly off-balance. The right ring is bent slightly more than the left.

BIT BALANCE

When we talk about balance for a Western curb bit, it means the leverage action of the bit rather than its manufacturing. The shape of a curb bit's shanks and the angle of the mouthpiece determine the balance. Although any bit must be well made, the balance of the curb determines the speed of tightening and release of the curb strap and how the leverage is applied to the poll. Rest the bit on your hand with the front of the bit facing away from you. Draw an imaginary line from the mouthpiece straight to the floor. When the bit is resting on your hand, note whether it floats toward you, floats away from you, or remains stable. That determines whether the bit is under or over balanced. It basically measures the weight of the shanks and angle in relationship to the mouthpiece.

The length and angle of the shanks determine the "balance" of the bit—in other words, how it rests in the horse's mouth.

Next, drape the bit over your index finger, letting each side of the link fall on either side of your finger. Do you feel any pinching? Do both sides of the bit feel identical on either side of your finger? If you're testing a double-jointed bit, such as a French snaffle or Dr. Bristol (see chapter 10), test each of the links.

For single-bar bits, such as a mullen mouth or a curb bit, simply rest the bit across the palm of your hand. Feel the weight. It should feel like one continuous piece of metal, with both sides the same weight. Run your finger over the entire length on all sides to check for rough spots or rough edges, particularly where the cheeks attach to the shanks or rings.

It's also wise to check on your bit after each use. We may look closely at a bit before we buy it, but then we attach it to the bridle, put it in the horse's mouth, and promptly forget about it. But bits wear, just like leather and other saddlery, and need regular inspection, cleaning, and polishing. After you rinse off your bit (which you should do after every ride), inspect the edges, the corners, and the finish. Note any irregular wear patterns or sharp edges. Less expensive bits and those that are plated, as well as those made of softer materials such as rubber, plastic, or copper, tend to wear more quickly than those made of stainless steel, sweet iron, German silver, or Aurigan.

As a horse owner, your quality control should be the same with synthetics, such as Nathe or vulcanite. Check your bit regularly for signs of wear, rubbing your fingers over it frequently. Wash it off after each ride, as the dried saliva and grass bits that accumulate in bits can cause decay.

THE CARE AND FEEDING OF YOUR BIT

Taking care of your bits properly will make them last a lot longer and ensure that they aren't hurting your horse with crustiness that can rub your horse's lips and cheeks.

When you buy a new bit, first wash it well in mild dish soap and warm water, making sure to rinse it thoroughly. Before you attach it to your bridle, give the bridle a good oiling, especially the loops that attach the bridle to the bit and the reins— these often get stiff from horse saliva and can dry and crack easily. It's crucial that these attachments are regularly checked to make sure the leather is holding its integrity. Also make sure your bridle is adjusted properly. Your cavesson noseband should rest no more than two fingers' width from the bottom of your horse's protruding cheekbone. For bridles without a noseband, the cheeks should not be so loose that pulling the sides away from the horse's face has no impact on the position of the bit. The bridle and bit adjustment should cause no more than two wrinkles in the corners of the horse's lips. Some Western bits are designed to be worn lower in the mouth, however, so adjust accordingly.

After each ride, dip the bit in clean water and rub the residue off with a towel or a soft sponge. Keep an old toothbrush

71

handy to clean out the joints and hinges. A plain piece of steel wool (not the kind infused with soap) helps to rub off rust or anything stuck on the bit. If you want your horse to have a little sweet rust taste on his metal bit, you might want to skip this last step. Wipe the bit dry with a clean cloth. Another method is to simply put your bit in the dishwasher and run it on the regular cycle. Also, if your bit rings squeak or lock, use an eyedropper or cotton swab to dab the moving parts with corn, olive, or vegetable oil. Now and then, polish your bits with a bit polish.

If you switch bits between different horses, or if you've been trading bits around the barn, set the dishwasher to "sanitize," or drop the bits in a pot of boiling water for five minutes. Always give the bit a really good cleaning after it's been in a different horse's mouth. Another quick way to disinfect a bit is to wash it with Listerine or other minty mouthwash that has bacteria-killing properties.

If you simply dip your bit in a bucket of clean water and rub it with your fingers or a soft sponge after every ride, and wash it in soap, water, and mouthwash when you do your regular tack cleaning routine, your bit won't collect any gunk in the joints and it will wear much longer.

It is long past time to retire this rubber bit.

CHAPTER - 9

CHEEKS AND RINGS

A bit's action is equal to the sum of its parts. In this chapter, we'll review the parts that remain outside the horse's mouth—the cheeks or the rings for snaffle bits, and the shanks for leverage bits.

Before we begin, let's consider the various overall types of bits and how they function. Bits are divided into four general families based on how they work:

- Direct contact bits: the snaffle
- Leverage bits: curbs, including Pelhams, Kimberwickes, and Western-style curbs
- Gag bits: elevators, bubble bits, and European gags
- Bitless: hackamores, mechanical hackamores, cross-under bridles, LG bridles, and rope halters

All these bits work on different parts of the head and mouth:

- Lips
- Bars
- Tongue
- Chin groove
- Poll
- Palate
- Cheeks (for some bitless models)

There's a lot of crossover within those four categories, but by and large, every bit you see can be grouped according to how it attaches to the headstall or bridle, the type of mouthpiece it has, and the kind of action it applies to the horse's head and mouth when pressure is applied. With combination bits coming into fashion, you may find one bit that fits into several categories depending on which parts of the apparatus you attach to the reins and how they apply pressure to the horse's head.

As we discussed, the bit is a tool used to communicate subtle signals to the horse. It isn't the steering wheel, although many people think so—the guiding of the horse comes through many different well-coordinated and timed signals. Turning the horse requires changing the balance of the seat, directing the body, and adding leg pressure. The well-trained horse and rider pair barely use the reins at all. Nonetheless, a bit, just like a carpenter's hammer, needs to be well made, balanced in the horse's mouth, and the correct size.

THE ANATOMY OF A BIT

The horse's anatomy; the rider's aids; the size and shape of the bit, the mouthpiece, and the bit rings; and the material from which it's made all factor in to the bit decision. While we'll talk about the four families in detail in chapter 10, you'll need to know the parts of the bit, and there is a common vocabulary. Just as you learned the parts of the horse, parts of a bridle, and so on, using the right words to describe pieces of the bit can help you identify which parts of the bit have the most impact on different parts of the horse.

Most bits consist of the cheek pieces, rings or shanks, the bit and bridle rings, and the mouthpiece. The different parts of a mouthpiece are called the canons. A canon is the part from the joint to the ring in a jointed bit, and from the middle of the port to the shank in a curb bit.

While we call the straps that attach the bit to the rest of the bridle "cheek pieces," the words "cheek" or "cheek piece" are also used to describe the part of the bit that is in contact with the horse's lower face. When the attachment between the bridle cheek piece and the bit is round, we usually refer to it as a bit ring. When it's straight, we might call it

a cheek piece, upper shank, or the purchase (for a leverage bit).

For most direct contact or snaffle bits, there are four basic families of bit rings, each with a different effect. Choosing the right bit has a lot to do with choosing the right bit rings.

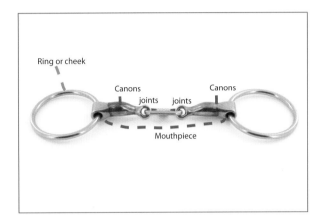

A bit consists of the cheeks or shanks, the joints (for linked bits), the canons, and the mouthpiece.

SNAFFLE BIT RINGS

Loose Rings

Loose rings are not "fixed" onto the canons of the bit. Instead, they are attached through holes drilled in the mouthpiece, sliding through the mouthpiece as well as the rein and bridle loops easily. The mouthpiece, if it is the correct size, moves both vertically and horizontally in the mouth. There is also just a fraction of an inch of "give" in the space between the mouthpiece and ring. When the rider takes up the reins, the vibration of the reins on the rings gives the signal that something is about to happen. Because both the mouthpiece and the reins

Loose Rings

The horse feels pressure from the bit on the lips, the cheeks, the poll and the nose, in addition to the pressure points inside of his mouth.

move on the rings, there is some play in a loose ring bit. Some loose ring proponents believe it is one of the best bits to try if you want your horse to salivate because of its overall flexibility. In general, the loose ring version is considered the "softer" version of most bits, because the impact of the rider's hands on the reins is diffused by the play in the rings and the movement of the mouthpiece. The rings themselves can be smaller, like those found in a bradoon (or bridoon); quite large; or anywhere in between. The rule of thumb is that the smaller the ring is, the less the bit moves in the mouth, and the more instantaneous the rein pressure. The wider the ring, the more steering advantage the rider has because of the pressure on the opposite cheek, but the more delayed the contact will be with the horse's mouth. One disadvantage of loose rings is that, if not fit correctly, rings moving through the holes in the canons can pinch the horse's lips.

Eggbutt, D-Ring, Full Cheek

In general, these three styles of cheeks are all attached to the mouthpieces through hinges. The mouthpiece doesn't move vertically on the rings. The canons are wider where they connect to the bit cheeks. They

have hinged, or swivel, cheeks, meaning you can use a direct rein to encourage a horse to turn because the ring moves away from the horse's face before the pressure on the outside ring is engaged. It also gives the rider the ability to ask for lateral flexion. As such, these three varieties of cheeks tend to work well for horses that don't turn well or need a slightly quicker direct rein action. When the rider applies direct rein to turn a horse, the bit's cheek applies more opposite cheek pressure than a loose ring. It will also be a more instantaneous sensation for the horse. Because the bit and the cheek are part of the same apparatus, there is no up-and-down play in the bit.

The eggbutt is shaped like an egg, with one side attached to the canons through either a hinge or a weld. The bit rings can swivel front and back but the mouthpiece is solidly attached and there is very little vertical play except through the positioning of the rider's hands. As the rider picks up the reins, the horse immediately feels the bit move in his mouth. The eggbutt offers a very direct contact and stability in the mouth. An eggbutt (as well as the D-ring and full cheek, below), is an excellent bit for younger horses who are insecure in their turning skills and their acceptance of

76

the contact. It's a steadier signal from the rider.

The D-ring has a straight bar attached to the canons and a D-shaped ring. It was originally a racing cheek but morphed into a general riding bit. It is quite popular among hunter/jumper and English pleasure riders. Like the eggbutt, it makes contact on the cheeks and has a steady feel in the mouthpiece with little vertical movement. In fact, the difference between the two has much more to do with fashion than with function. The D-ring, because of the straightness of the piece that lies against the horse's face, is also an excellent bit to reinforce steering. The reins have more slide with a D-ring than with an eggbutt since the ring is rounder, but the cheeks are straighter, giving the horse more turning security. Also, in many D-rings, the rings themselves are rounded rather than flat.

The bit ring with the most ability to influence the horse's steering is the full

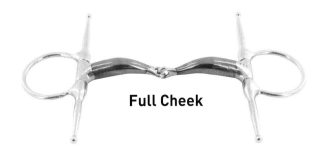

Full Cheek

cheek. It has straight cheek pieces that run an inch or more above and below the mouthpiece, with a solid ring to attach to the reins. The full cheek is an excellent bit for younger horses who may not understand steering, because there is much surface area next to the horse's cheek. With full cheek snaffles, it is very important that the tops of the cheeks have keepers on them to hold them in place. Otherwise they can poke the horse's nose or get caught on shirts, fences, or other protruding objects. The full cheek is a very popular and effective bit. The attachment of the tops of the cheeks to the bridle gives this bit a degree of poll leverage as well.

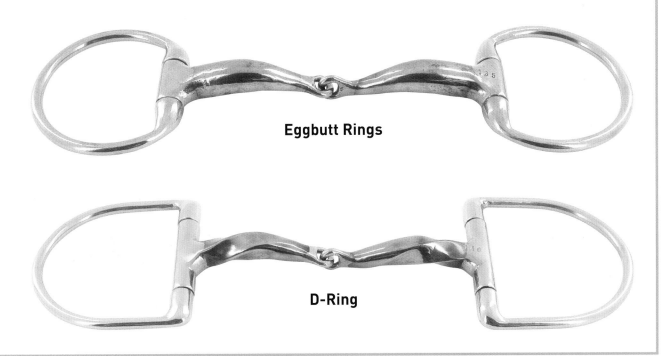

Eggbutt Rings

D-Ring

Fulmer

The Fulmer cheek is a full cheek with a loose ring instead of a fixed ring. The Fulmer combines the advantages of the fixed cheek with those of the loose ring. Because the rings aren't welded solidly onto the cheek pieces, it provides a little more play in the rein contact but has the steering power of the full cheek. It's an excellent bit for those who want more lateral control but prefer a little softer option with more subtle signals. The keepers on the bridle can, if used correctly, provide just a little leverage pressure similar to a very light curb bit.

With all the hinged ring bits described above, horses that lean on the bit will find a solid place on which to rest their heads.

Loose rings discourage the horse from resting on the contact instead of carrying his head and neck himself, provided he is working properly over his topline. D-rings, eggbutts, and full-cheeks are most popular in the hunter ring, where jaw flexion isn't as necessary as a soft, forward carriage. Western riders who use direct rather than neck reining like D-rings and loose rings (which they call O-rings).

Baucher, Hanging Snaffle, B-Ring

The Baucher cheek, hanging snaffle, and fillis are all the different names for a single bit. While in theory these bits are direct contact, the extra length of the cheek created

Fulmer

To understand what happens to a horse's head when using a leverage bit, simulate the action by pulling back on the bottom rings. The bridle rings go forward and downward at the same time. This places pressure on the poll and presses the mouthpiece against the tongue.

Photo by: Dusty Perin

by the distance from the bridle ring to the rein ring adds an element of poll pressure to bits with these cheeks.

For the sake of this book, we'll use "Baucher" to describe a bit with two round rings: one very small ring attached to the cheek pieces of the bridle, and the other, larger ring attached to the reins and the canons. This style of cheek, named after Francois Baucher, the controversial nineteenth-century French riding master, is suspended slightly above the tongue and below the palate. When rein contact is applied, the bit applies pressure on the bars of the mouth and the cheek attachments pull slightly downward, applying pressure on the horse's poll. Because there is some length between the cheek piece attachment and the main ring, this bit has a slight leverage action in the same way the full cheek attached to the cheek pieces with keepers has some poll pressure to help encourage flexion and roundness.

From the trotting and driving worlds come the half- and full-spoon cheek. While not very popular for saddle horses these days, the half-spoon is still used in trotting and driving circles. Just as it sounds, the half-spoon has a small bar hanging downward from the bit ring and it has a flattened out end like a spoon. The full spoon has pieces above and below the mouthpiece. Their action is very similar to the full cheek, but without the pointy ends and the keepers. The full spoon does not have any leverage.

Within these categories of cheeks are many variations in length and width. No matter the size, width, or shape, all snaffle cheeks are very much variations on the following theme: when the rider applies pressure on the rein, the horse feels it directly on his mouth. There is little pressure on the poll and none on the chin groove because snaffle bits lack curb straps. That's one of the reasons the Baucher, while applying some pressure, is not a true leverage bit.

SHANKS AND LEVERAGE CHEEKS

As we saw in the historical section of this book, the shank has been around almost as long as the horse has been domesticated. Early riders figured out that poll pressure brought the horse's head down, which made him easier to control. This was especially true for early chariot horses, and thus some of the first shanked bits were developed for this use.

Understanding how and when to use shanked and leverage bits requires both a minor knowledge of physics and an understanding of basic horse anatomy. Whether they are short or long, English or Western style, the laws of physics apply.

Consider this: The reins are attached *below* the mouthpiece, while the cheeks are attached to the cheek pieces of the bridle *above* the mouthpiece. If you rest the mouthpiece in the palm of your hand with the front of the bit facing away from you,

The flexed Western bridle horse is ridden with a loose rein until correction is needed. The length of the shanks determines the amount of leverage.

and pull the rein rings back as if you were applying rein contact, the upper shanks come forward and the mouthpiece swivels forward in your palm.

This action is called the "balance" of the bit. The shape and angle of the shanks will often change the balance. If you draw an imaginary straight line from the mouthpiece to the ground, notice if the bit is straight up and down, tilted forward, or tilted backward against that imaginary line.

The majority of English shanked bits— Pelhams and Weymouths, for example—are straight balanced. As the shank curves back, the balance shifts as well. Flat, rather than round, bridle rings also help a bit's balance because the cheek pieces of the bridle are

more securely fastened and do not slide after the action is engaged.

Given that the upper ring is attached to the cheek pieces, which are then attached to or are part of the crownpiece of the bridle, the action of pulling back on the reins pulls the crown piece down against the horse's poll. Simultaneously, the curb strap, which rests loosely in the horse's chin groove, is tightened against the horse's skin by the forward rotation of the upper rings and the mouthpiece.

In general, curb bits have two or sometimes three loops through which to attach the reins. The angle and the length of the shank determine the severity of the bit and the amount of "signal" the horse receives

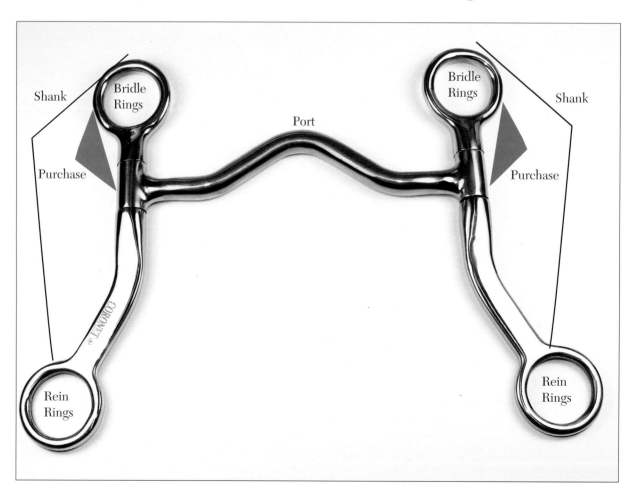

before he feels the full effects of the curb strap, mouth pressure, and poll pressure. The shanks can be fixed or they can be hinged (or "loose jawed" in Western) which allows more lateral flexibility. More advanced reining horse trainers or riders tend to like the lateral action of the hinged shanks more than the fixed shank, which has no flexibility when sideways pressure is applied.

The shanked bit has three important measurements. The first is the length of the shank overall. The second is the length of the shank from the mouthpiece to the bottom of the shanks, where the rein rings are located. The third is the length of shank from the mouthpiece to the bridle cheek piece attachments. The smaller the distance between the top of the shanks and the mouthpiece, the quicker the action of the bit. This is called the purchase—from the mouthpiece to the bridle attachment.

The amount of pressure, the quickness of the bit's response to rein pressure, and the time it takes to engage the curb strap or chain varies from bit to bit by the ratio of the length of the lower shanks to the upper shanks.

The curb strap or chain can be made of various materials with differing uses. In the English arena, it's most common to see a curb chain. Just like bits, curb chains have varying levels of severity, from mild to more severe. The single-link curb chain is one of the more serious options, but it's largely gone out of fashion. On English bridles, double bridles, and bits such as the Kimberwicke, the chain of choice has double-links, which make it much softer since the links form a relatively smooth surface. Curb chains

have a single link that dangles off the center, through which you can slip a lip strap (sometimes called a bit hobble in the Western arena). The lip strap prevents the horse from grabbing the shanks of the bit. It doesn't apply to all bits—you primarily find lip strap attachments on Pelhams and Weymouths, but not all bits have that extra loop, and not all curb chains have a place to slide the lip strap through. At the sides of the chain are three or four links that allow the chain to be tightened or loosened on the hooks that lie close to the mouthpiece. The dangling link in the center clues the rider as to whether or not the chain is centered. The chain must lie absolutely flat against the horse's chin groove. To do this you have to twist the chain until all the links are lying flat against each other.

Curb chains come in varying link lengths. The flat link chain is a single-link chain that covers a wider area. Thin chains are more severe than thick chains. Some riders prefer the chain, but will cover it with a rubber or gel curb guard to soften the contact with the chin groove. The extra links can be snipped off, or simply left to hang there, although they could very well get caught on something.

The Western curb bit is more likely to use a leather strap than a chain, although either is an option. The properly adjusted curb strap on a Western bit should lie two fingers' width between the strap and the horse. A too-tight strap may either numb your horse's reaction or incite him to argue with you. A too-loose strap is ineffective. A chain in Western tack is usually attached with leather loops. Some Western riders do

83

twist their chains for a quicker response, but this is illegal at horse shows. If you need to twist your curb chain, you might consider a different bit or better training. A trained Western horse will be light in the bridle and won't have any need for the extra "reminder" of the curb chain.

For both Western and English horses, the curb bit applies pressure to the poll and to the tongue, bars, and lips.

How Leverage Bits Work

Contrary to the snaffle, the curb applies indirect pressure on three different points. As the rider makes contact with the reins, the horse feels pressure on his poll, his mouth (through the bit), and his chin (through the curb strap).

- The shorter the shank, the quicker the horse feels the rein pressure.
- Straight shanks are quicker than S-shaped or curved "grazer" shanks.
- The longer the shank, the *less* rein pressure is needed to signal the horse.
- The ratio of purchase to lower shank determines the ounces of pressure the horse feels on the chin groove and the poll. For example, a one-inch purchase and a four-inch lower shank produce a 1:3 ratio—or three ounces of pressure on the properly adjusted curb strap for every one ounce of rein pressure from the rider. That same bit has 1:4 ratio of purchase to full shank, thus four ounces of pressure on the bit in the horse's mouth for every one ounce placed on the reins.

A long lower shank in relation to the upper shank (or purchase) increases the leverage, and thus the pressure, on the chin groove where the curb strap is resting and on the bars of the mouth. A long upper shank in relation to the lower shank increases the pressure on the poll, but does not apply as much pressure on the bars of the mouth.

In Western bits, it's not uncommon to see very, very long shanks on horses that seem quite light in the bridle, with arched necks and heads perpendicular to the ground. Note that those shanks are used, at this stage of training, in very delicate ways—a slight lift of the hand in conjunction with a leg and seat cue instantly signals the horse and puts him quickly into position. These long-shanked bits are not for beginner riders or for green horses and should be used with great care and caution.

In the English-style leverage bits, such as the Pelham and the Weymouth, there are frequently two sets of reins—one attached to a direct-contact bit. In the Pelham, that's just a direct rein loop on the shank, and with the Weymouth, meant to be used with a double bridle, there's a snaffle bit in the horse's mouth as well. The leverage is applied quickly and judiciously through the use of a second rein, while the snaffle contact is more constant. Most English leverage bits tend to be shorter shanked, and thus the leverage action is very quick and less forceful than in the long-shanked, single rein Western versions.

The Kimberwicke falls into its own category because it is a hybrid leverage and snaffle bit. It is used with a single rein, and it comes with two different kinds of cheeks: one is a regular D-shaped ring, and the other is slotted. The slotted version is called the Uxeter. Both types of Kimberwickes are leverage bits because they have a curb chain that engages as the rider applies rein contact. The closer the rein is to the mouthpiece, the less fulcrum action there is, and the less leverage. So, when the bit is attached to a regular, non-slotted cheek piece, it has very little leverage because the reins are connected directly to the mouthpiece. A slight upward motion of the hands engages the leverage through the tightening of the curb chain.

English leverage bits and bridles often come with two sets of reins, giving the rider the option of working with just the snaffle while letting the leverage rein remain slack until needed. Note that the chain hook should be on the other side of the bit ring, close to the face.

Like a Pelham, the Kimberwicke uses the action of the curb chain to engage some leverage. Above, a D-ring Kimberwicke with less leverage.

On the slotted version, you can choose a direct rein or a leverage rein. The lower slot on the ring produces the most leverage on the poll and indirect pressure on the bars.

This leverage action is slightly different from that of the Western curb. Primarily because English riders like to feel more contact with the bit and train their horses thusly, many English-style curb bits apply more direct bit pressure through the snaffle rein, giving the rider the option of only using the curb or leverage rein when they need it, letting the rein lie slack against the horse's neck the rest of the time. Sometimes this is accomplished by having the rider hold a steady but light contact with both the snaffle and the curb, applying a little more wrist action to activate the curb or to remind the horse to balance as needed. There are also several options for how to hold both sets of reins—they can cross each other, or they can be straight from mouthpiece to hand. The choice is largely based on rider preference, but does have an impact on how quickly the horse feels the action of the curb and

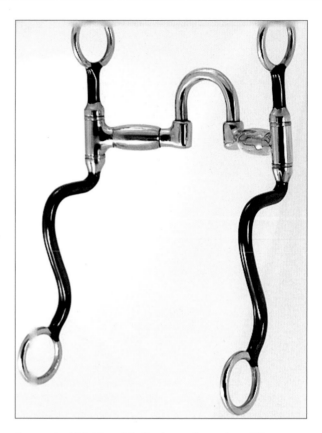

An angled bit like this S-shaped version diffuses the leverage, making it less severe than a straight-shanked curb.

what the rider needs to do with his hands to engage it.

Shank Shapes

Western shanks can be the canvases upon which metal artists express themselves. Shanks have been decorated with a great variety of shapes, styles, and icons for thousands of years.

In general, Western shanks come in the following shapes:

Curved grazer shanks: They curve back toward the horse. Their original purpose was to stay out of the way of the ground as the working cow horse grazed. They also stay out of the way of the rope as the cowboy throws it toward a cow.

The angle of the shanks means they stay out of the way of the working cowboy's ropes, and allow the horse to graze during downtime.

Photo by: Dusty Perin

The rider in this photo is taking a little more contact, as evidenced by the angle of the shanks. The reins are heavy enough that the rider has to do very little with his hands for the horse to feel it in his mouth.

The 7-shaped shank has slightly more leverage than the S-shaped, because it has straighter shanks.

S-shaped: These are also frequently found in Western bits and driving bits and have several purposes. One is to soften the leverage. The second is to keep the shanks away from the horse's mouth. S-shaped shanks also tend to be more decorative than straight shanks.

7-shaped: Similar to an S-shaped shank, these shanks assure the horse won't be able to grab the shank in his mouth. The angle of the shank diffuses the leverage on the poll and chin.

Driving shanks: Although we have not spent much time on driving or racing bits in this book so far, it is worth mentioning that many of the bits we use today were first developed for use with carriage horses. Driving bits have the same general

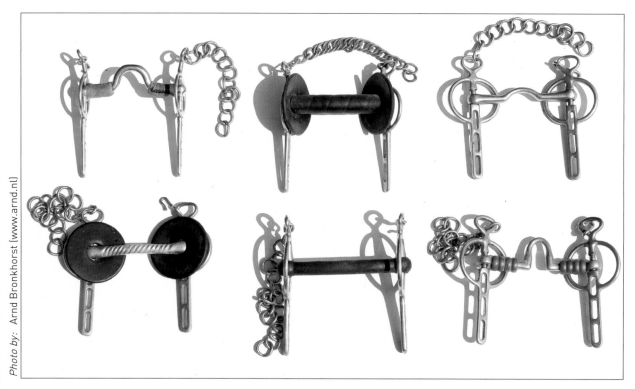

Photo by: Arnd Bronkhorst (www.arnd.nl)

Driving bits such as these Liverpools have straight shanks with many slots for different rein connections and leverage strength.

mouthpiece selections as riding bits. The shanks in a Liverpool-style carriage bit are long, straight, and slotted to accommodate multiple rein sets.

Other driving shanks include the elbow, similar to the 7-shank, and the Buxton, which is similar to an S-shaped shank. Both have a rein ring and two slots.

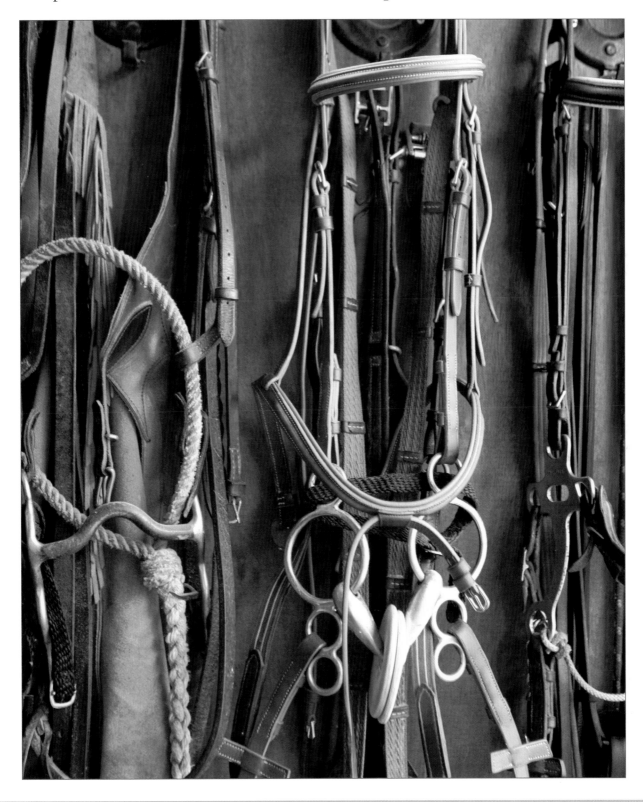

CHAPTER - 10

MOUTHPIECES

"For the experienced rider who has mastered the independent seat and the soft, sensitive rein contact, the question of which bit and bridle to use is of little importance."

—Gerhard Kapitzke

If you knew nothing about bits and were forced to buy a new one for some reason or another, you'd be stunned by the variety and potentially overwhelmed by the choice.

While such a plethora of bits means we have plenty of options for trial and error, it doesn't necessarily mean there's a "silver bullet" answer for our riding and training problems. As we've mentioned earlier in this book, bitting a horse is a training matter, not an equipment matter.

Nonetheless, a thorough knowledge of bits and an ability to sort them out is essential to good horsemanship. If, as we postulate, an experienced rider needs only a well-developed sense of timing, a fine seat with refined leg aids, and an understanding of rein contact, the bit becomes a little beside the point. It's there to help us refine our ride,

or give the horse a reminder with a slightly stronger aid.

It may help to use a different bit as you advance your training and would like to add more finesse and lightness to your ride. In fact, several disciplines, particularly Western bridle horses and dressage horses, switch bits as they move up the training scale. Of all the bits out there, remember: Gadgets don't fix training problems. Riders fix training problems.

While it may appear that each bit comes in a dizzying array of sizes, cheek pieces, and so forth, there are actually a relatively limited number of styles. If you understand the function of each of the different mouthpieces

There are so many bits on the market today, it's easy to get overwhelmed. If you remember, however, that bits come in families, it makes the decision process easier.

his gums and how his lips and cheeks look inside and out, and feel inside his mouth to determine how thick his tongue is and how far from the top of his mouth it is when it's lying softly on his mouth.

And don't forget that a bit's action is the sum of its parts. A horse may like a certain mouthpiece but may actually go better with different cheeks. Bridle fit, noseband, tightness of the curb strap, and the position of the bit in the mouth also play a role. While there are "rules" about bit fit and size, the key is understanding that each horse's mouth and preferences are different, so work with your horse, not with the rules.

For example, bit makers and researchers have discovered the faultiness of the common wisdom that the thicker the bit, the milder it is. Some researchers have found that a thick bit in a horse with a small mouth and a thick tongue may actually feel more severe to that horse than a similar style in a smaller width. It may be uncomfortable enough for him to want to fight with it in much the same way he would a too-thin bit. Also, our perception of the angle of the bit in the mouth has changed, and bit makers have experimented with angling the mouthpieces so they lie against the tongue in different ways. Some bits are angled forward in the horse's mouth, some have pieces that are angled backward, and some have a combination of the two.

Another key point is that different styles of mouthpieces should be sized differently. European-made models, for example, may be slightly larger or smaller than the noted size in inches because the millimeters-to-inches conversion isn't exact. Bits with a loose ring

and shanks, you can put together the pieces for a bit that might help your horse.

Before choosing your bit, understand the differences in bit bar widths and how they have an impact on your horse's mouth. Also, as we described in the anatomy section, take time to explore the inside of your horse's mouth. Get to know the normal color of

94

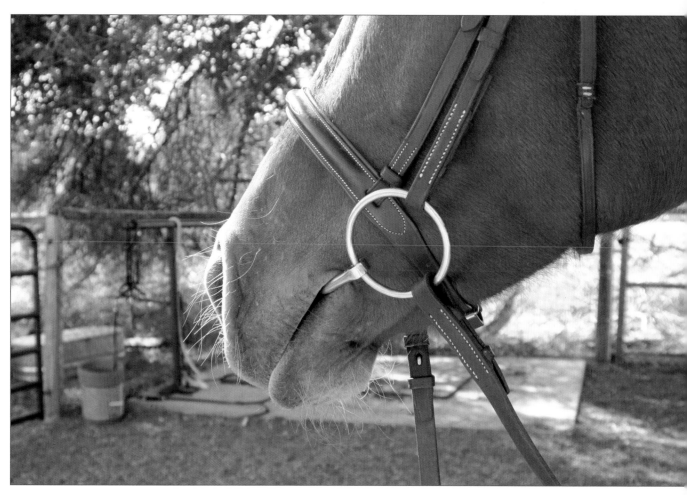

This bit is too long for this delicate mare's mouth.

should fit a little wider in the mouth than those with a fixed ring to prevent pinching. There are now different kinds of devices to measure bits, from Sprenger's measuring kit that measures both the size of the mouth and the proper width of the bit bars, to the plastic "Bit Fit" that fits in your horse's mouth and allows you to adjust the wheels on either side of his face to determine the size of your bit. You can also experiment, if your tack store will let you, with different sizes of bits. If you don't want to pay a fortune to purchase a bunch of bits, ask friends to borrow bits of different sizes and styles. Disinfect the bits with Listerine before you return them.

Bits come in a variety of lengths and are measured in two different ways. Lengths of the mouthpieces are generally expressed in inches in the United States and run from 3 ¼ inches (for ponies) to 7 inches (for draft horses). The bit size for an average adult horse is usually between 4 ¾ and 5 ¼ inches. Nonetheless, many horses have abnormally narrow or wide mouths, so be sure to measure. Nicole Polligkeit, a master trainer from Germany who offers clinics for dressage and jumper riders in the United States, noted that she almost always finds at least two or three bits that don't fit during her clinics.

The size of the mouthpiece (as stated on the store tag) is measured from the inside of one cheek piece to the inside of the other. To know if the mouthpiece fits, place your index finger sideways between the ring and the horse's cheek. It should fit without too much slack or pressure. If the horse's "smile"—his lip wrinkles—increases substantially when you slide your finger in between the cheek and the horse, the bit may be too tight. Having such a tight bit basically negates any action the bit might have. It puts constant pressure on the tongue, the bars, and the lips.

For curb bits, you'll also need to know the three measurements mentioned in chapter 9, as the shank lengths determine the quickness of the fulcrum action and severity of the leverage.

Other measurements to consider are the diameter (thickness) of the mouthpiece and the bit rings. The mouthpiece is measured at its widest point, which is where it attaches to the cheek pieces or rings. Diameter is generally expressed in centimeters. The rings on a loose ring, D-ring, or eggbutt may also be measured from the top to the bottom of the ring.

Ideally, there should be ½ to ¾ inch of clearance between the lips and the ring—approximately the width of your index finger.

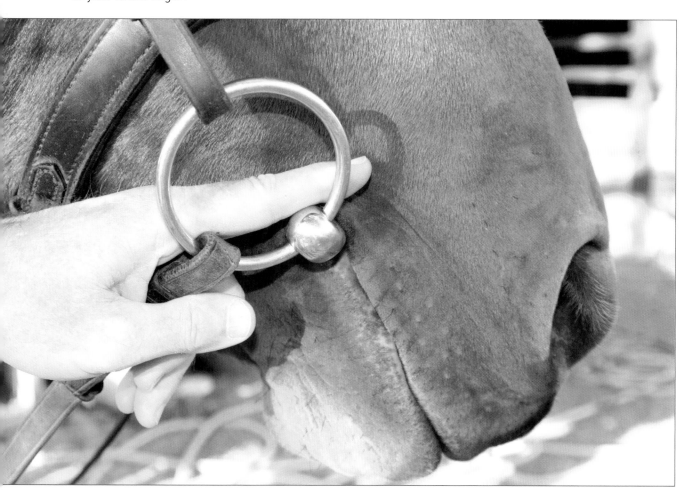

Devices like the Bit Fit can help you take an accurate measure of your horse's mouth.

A bit that's hanging properly in a horse's mouth should leave no more than two wrinkles at the corners.

Bits can be divided into four broad categories—direct contact bits, leverage bits, gag bits, and bitless bridles. Even though it helps to categorize them thusly, there are many more that don't fit into any single family because they're a combination of several types of bits. For example, the combination hackamore is a "nose bridle" that also has a bit. The Mikmar combination bit has a mouthpiece, a nose string, and direct and leverage bitting options. So while bit and bridle academicians have developed these neat categories, bit design and development advances have made them somewhat obsolete.

Nonetheless, we'll divide them in the traditional way, noting those that don't fall cleanly into any of the categories.

Every one of these bits can be misused in the wrong hands, whether or not it is considered a harsh or severe bit. Some of the harshest *looking* bits can actually be quite gentle in the right hands. Other bits *are* harsh in any hands and should never have been invented. After all, if a horse needs a bicycle chain in his mouth, he needs a new rider and trainer.

THE SNAFFLE

The most common bit today, the snaffle is a direct contact bit. That means that the reins attach to the rings, which are directly attached to the mouthpiece. Pull on the rein and the bit moves. The word snaffle comes from the German word for beak, or nose,

Measure rings inside

Measure mouthpiece from inside of rings

Measure width of mouthpiece at widest point

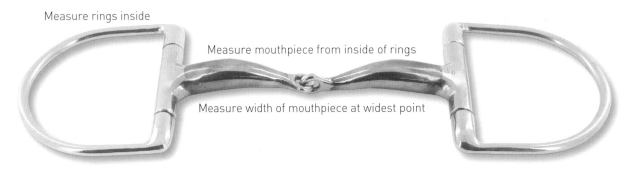

Measure the mouthpiece from inside each ring or shank. Note that European-made bits will not measure exactly in inches because they are sized using metric measurements.

Luckily, the only version of this cruel bicycle chain bit the author was able to find is a very old, obviously retired model, although they are still sold in some places.

Schnabel, or the more archaic version, *snavel*, circa 1533. Snaffle can refer to the direct contact bit, but the word itself is also used synonymously with the simple direct contact bridle in some English riding circles. Snaffle bit mouthpieces come in many shapes—they may be straight, curved, ported, jointed, double-jointed, plastic, rubber, metal core with rubber covering, or any variation thereof. They can also come with any of the snaffle cheek pieces mentioned in chapter 9.

What makes a snaffle a snaffle is not the mouthpiece, but the action of the reins. When the rider pulls on the reins, the horse feels it in his mouth. Where that pressure is located depends on the mouthpiece and cheeks in combination. For the most part, the pressure is on the corners of the lips, the bars, and the tongue. That's what differentiates it from its fellow bits—not the rings, the mouthpiece, the width, or the size. (see Bitting Myths and Misconceptions, page 128). The rider's use of the reins also has an

impact on the pressure points. If the rider lifts his hands *up* instead of pulling back, the bit presses on the lips. A lower hand puts more pressure on the bars.

The action of a snaffle is relatively simple to understand. When the bit is at rest in the horse's mouth, it lays across the tongue. The edges of the bit make contact with the lips and rest lightly on the bars. If the bridle is fit correctly, the horse will have two wrinkles at the corners of his lips. The bit will be located in the inter-dental space between the front incisors and the back molars. Depending on the mouthpiece, the bit drapes on the tongue.

The basic snaffle's most important attribute is that it offers the rider the ability to use a direct rein and give the horse signals to increase his lateral flexibility. The amount of that flexibility varies greatly according to the mouthpiece. A solid mouthpiece such as a straight bar or ported mouthpiece has much less lateral flexibility than a double-jointed mouthpiece, for example. Still, the snaffle is an excellent all-purpose style that can be used from first bridling to last.

Like the families of cheek pieces, bit mouthpieces have their unique attributes.

Single-Jointed Mouthpiece

It used to be one of the most common bits. Every horse owner seemed to have a single-jointed D-ring or eggbutt snaffle in his or her tack box. While this bit was likely invented centuries ago and is still common, the single-jointed snaffle has a couple of drawbacks.

As the rider picks up the rein contact, the joint folds across the tongue. It forms an upside-down V shape in the mouth, and the canons press down on the bars of the mouth. Simultaneously, the angle of the bit sharpens. The joint pokes toward the roof of the mouth while the canons squeeze the jaw.

A thick, single-jointed snaffle bit was for many years considered the mildest of all bits because it was believed that it spread the pressure across the mouth relatively evenly. However, researchers have used mouth X-rays to discover that the single-jointed snaffle bit is not quite as benign as once thought.

Imagine a nutcracker: When you place the walnut inside the two arms and squeeze, the angle of the nutcracker squeezes two sides of the nut and causes it to crack. And that described the potential problem with a single-jointed bit in a, *ahem*, nutshell.

Not all riders and snaffle bits cause this problem—the single-jointed snaffle is a perfectly effective and soft bit in the right hands. However, if the rider has hands that constantly pull, a single-jointed snaffle can turn into a much harsher bit than many people realize. This bit style is less severe in the hands of a rider who converses with the horse's mouth, taking and releasing. The release of the reins softens the angle of the canons and mitigates the squeezing of the jaw.

As such, a properly used single-jointed snaffle can be an effective all-purpose bit. The proper fit is also important to avoid the damaging "nutcracker" action. If the bit is

99

◀A snaffle bit is one in which pressure on the reins causes a direct impact on the mouthpiece of the bit.

This horse is protesting contact—the open mouth and disturbed expression signify that perhaps this single-jointed snaffle doesn't feel quite right.

too small, it will pinch the corners of the horse's mouth and lips, and may lead to sores if used incorrectly. If the bit is too wide, the nutcracker effect is exacerbated by extra length and is more likely to poke the palate and bruise the bars.

The single-jointed snaffle should have just enough room between the lips and

bridle and sliding the bit gently through the mouth so it is even.

The bit rings will have an impact on the play and effect of the single-jointed snaffle. The full-cheek, eggbutt, and D-ring don't allow much vertical play in the bit. A solid bit ring allows a quicker communication conduit to your horse and is "sharper" than a loose ring, which has much more play in it.

The single-jointed D-ring, eggbutt, or full-cheek snaffle are particularly effective for horses that may have trouble turning and for young horses who need to feel "cause and effect" before graduating to a lighter bit. The loose ring has more flexibility. It is very useful for most light horses who already know the basics.

Western riders who use a snaffle tend to prefer thin, single-jointed mouthpieces with a loose or D-ring cheek. It's quite rare to find an eggbutt in the Western arena. Western riders have also embraced the shaped mouthpiece of the Myler bits, which are curved, following the arc of the tongue.

While jointed snaffles are considered soft and gentle bits, there are a number of severe versions that should only be used briefly, if at all, under the supervision of a trainer. These mouthpieces come in a variety of materials but share a common theme: When contact is applied to the reins, the effect is sharp against the tongue.

Twisted mouthpieces: These look identical to a single-jointed snaffle, but instead of a smooth surface, the metal

the bit rings that you can slide a finger on each side. Also, make sure that your bridle is adjusted evenly and there is an equal amount of bit on either side of the horse's mouth. You may have to look at your horse from the front, adjusting the sides of the

102

If you look closely, you can see that this bit is not straight in the horse's mouth.

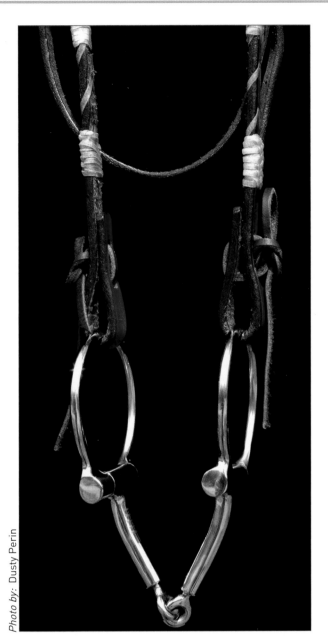

Photo by: Dusty Perin

Western riders prefer the D-ring, with a thinner mouthpiece.

today. It is both very thin and very sharp. It is second only to a double-twisted wire, in which the mouthpiece is actually two separate, single-link, single-twisted wire mouthpieces. This is an extremely severe family of bits, and if you think you need one of these, you probably need a trainer who can help you restart your horse. Double-mouthpiece-linked bits, such as the W-mouth or the double-twisted wire, can trap the tongue between the two mouthpieces and cause pinching. To add to the potential seriousness of these bits, you can actually

English leverage bits and bridles often come with two sets of reins, giving the rider the option of working with just the snaffle while letting the leverage rein remain slack until needed.

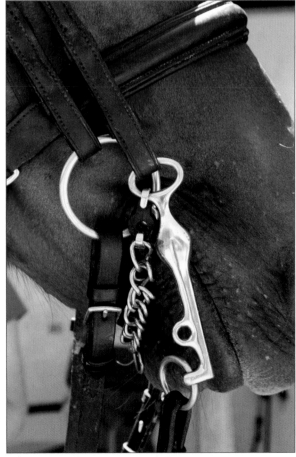

has a twist that adds sharp edges. The slow twist has a wider surface and is therefore somewhat less severe than those with very thin mouthpieces and those with more twist—called a fast twist.

Wire mouthpieces: A single-twisted wire snaffle is one of the most severe direct contact bits on the market

The double mouthpiece of this bit is relatively unfriendly to the bars and the tongue. It can easily pinch the tongue, poke the roof of the mouth, and exacerbate the "nutcracker" effect of a single-jointed snaffle.

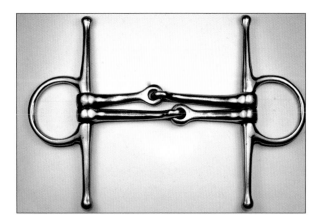

poke the palate with two mouthpieces instead of one.

Myler bits: Among the newer inventions in single-jointed bits are the Myler mouthpieces, which are curved to follow the shape of the mouth, but much thinner. The theory is that the thinner mouthpiece and the curved angle provide more tongue relief than traditional bits. They also feature several unique takes on

the Dick Christian and the Dr. Bristol. One interesting element of Myler bits is the way the rings are attached: To prevent the pinching that loose rings can cause, the company has designed a tubular attachment that protects the lips yet still allows the ring to move on the mouthpiece.

Double-Jointed Mouthpiece

The double-jointed snaffle is a very good alternative to the nutcracker effect of the single-jointed mouthpiece. The double-jointed snaffle lies across the tongue, resting in a natural arc. It is considered a gentle bit, although that depends on the shape and angle of the center link. When the rider pulls up on the reins, the bit flexes and increases pressure on the horse's lips. When the rider pulls back on the reins, the bit conforms to the horse's tongue shape, and that's where he feels the pressure.

The double-jointed snaffle is fit in the same manner as the single-jointed bit. There should be no more than a finger's width between the cheek and the bit ring. Because the bit is looser in the horse's mouth, there's

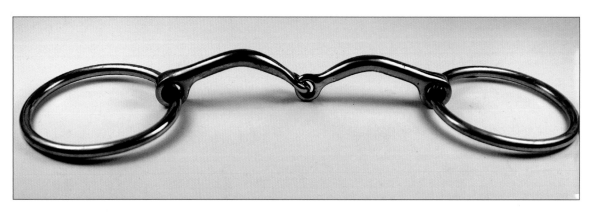

The curved canons of the Myler bit are reputed to be softer on the tongue and bars than a normal single-link snaffle.

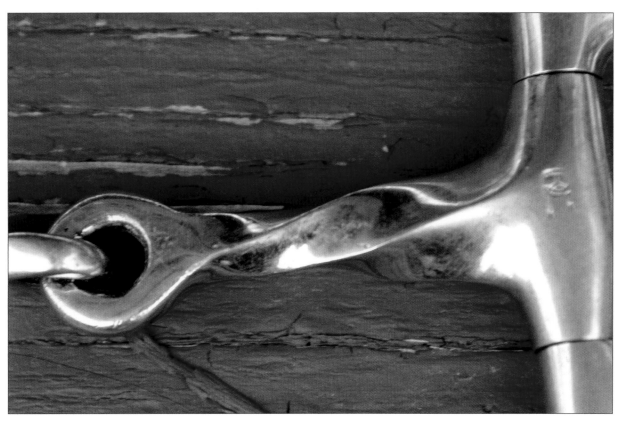

The sharp edges of this slow-twist mouthpiece are hard on the horse's tongue.

much more give in the entire apparatus. The double-jointed snaffle applies more pressure against the lips and the tongue, but less pressure on the bars. Double-jointed snaffles are particularly popular with dressage riders because they tend to invite horses to accept the bit more readily, while at the same time discouraging them from leaning on the bit or becoming too heavy because the mouthpiece has so much flexibility.

These days, many Western trainers also choose the double-jointed snaffle for starting horses. A double-jointed snaffle is an excellent, all-around choice for any well-trained, direct-reined horse.

Double-jointed snaffles can cause different reactions in the horse's mouth depending on the size, shape, and angle of the middle piece. A smooth piece that's more or less the same shape as the rest of the bit is one of the most comfortable and well-designed options on the market today. It's comfortable for the horse because it forms a single, smooth, and yet very flexible surface that follows the shape of the horse's tongue. The flexibility encourages the horse to play with the bit and release his jaw.

Double-jointed snaffles come with a variety of shapes in the center pieces. This is a lozenge double-jointed snaffle from Sprenger.

This loose-ring spinner is designed to help the horse keep his tongue under the bit.

When a rider pulls on the reins attached to a double-jointed snaffle, the bit rotates on its axis and slides back along the tongue. There is very little pressure on the sensitive bones of the jaw or on the roof of the mouth.

The double-jointed snaffle bit comes with a variety of link options in the middle. This can be a simple figure-eight-shaped plate—Western riders call it a dog bone—that attaches to each side of the canons, or it can be a "lozenge" or a bead that is shaped like an olive. Other choices include a small rubber ball or a copper barrel (sometimes called a cricket) that spins when the horse plays with it. These latter two options entice the horse to move his tongue, which signals him to produce saliva and soften his jaw.

A double-jointed mouthpiece can also have a metal ring (a Dick Christian) or two metal rings in the shape of a figure-eight. Sprenger makes a double-jointed bit with a small disk in the center of the middle lozenge that rolls—particularly effective for horses that tend to lock their jaws and tongues in place, lack softness, and don't chew. The disk gives the horse something to play with.

Some of these bits now have a center lozenge that's offset at a 45-degree angle or made of a different material. The effect this has is to make the joint roll to match the angle of the tongue as the rider takes up contact. Some unique styles of double-jointed snaffles are described below.

Dr. Bristol: This bit has a long, rectangular plate in the center instead of a

The Dr. Bristol's center plate is angled so the edge presses on the tongue when the bit is engaged. It is slightly stronger than a French link.

106

Unlike the Dr. Bristol, the French link has a figure-8-shaped center. It is sometimes called a "dog bone."

lozenge. Because of the length and relative sharpness of the edge of this plate, the Dr. Bristol tends to have more "bite"—or sharpness—than those bits with a rounded ball, bean, or lozenge in the center. When the reins are applied, the plate's edge presses down on the tongue. When the reins are soft, the plate rests across the surface of the tongue.

French link: A mouthpiece that's frequently confused with the Dr. Bristol is the French link (also called a dog bone). The two are quite different. The French link has a figure-eight-shaped plate in the middle with beveled edges and very large holes through which the canons are attached. Because of its shape, the French link has less flat surface area on the tongue than the Dr. Bristol. The center portion of a French link is angled 45 degrees from the canons. When the reins are passive, the mouthpiece rests across the tongue, but when the rider takes up contact, the mouthpiece rotates, and the link lies flat on the tongue. The French link is considered a gentler bit than the Dr. Bristol.

Dick Christian: One of the harsher variations of the double-jointed snaffle is the Dick Christian bit, in which the lozenge is replaced by a ring that lies on the tongue. The Dick Christian is a relatively rare bit found mostly in the U.K. It has an "edge" like the Dr. Bristol, but the ring might discourage a horse from putting his tongue over the bit.

Single Bar Mouthpieces

Single bar mouthpieces are made from a single piece of metal or rubber and do not have any links. While they may seem

The angle of the center plate causes it to lie flat against the tongue when the reins are tightened.

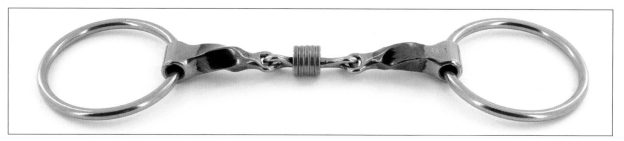

Brass rings help the horse to accept the bit, salivate, and soften in the mouth.

harsher than linked snaffle bits, that's not necessarily true. Like linked bits, they come in various widths, shapes, and materials, and with a wide variety of cheek pieces. Some bar mouth bits have ports, or upside down U's, in the center. They can be made of rubber, vulcanite, or Nathe, or metals such as copper, Aurigan, or stainless steel. In fact, a rubber bar mouth with flexibility is considered one of the softest bits available, and it may be preferable to some jointed bits in its taste and gentle action.

Mullen mouth: This is one of the most common of the single bar snaffles. It has a slight bow to it, allowing room for the tongue, and it applies a diffused pressure over the tongue, the bars, and the lips. The mullen mouth comes in all the usual materials. In its snaffle form it is considered a fairly mild bit. As with most single-bar mouthpieces, the mullen mouth

A copper mullen mouth gives the horse stability, but not a lot of encouragement to flex laterally.

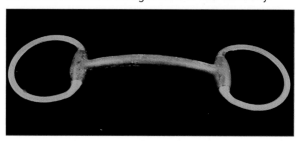

doesn't encourage much flexion in the horse's jaw. The mullen mouth is a common bit for driving horses, where independent movement of either side of the horse's mouth isn't as necessary as straightness to the contact. Rubber mullen mouths work very well for horses who are very sensitive to metal. The rubber is thick enough that it provides a comfortable cushion against the tongue, while the flexibility allows give and play in the mouthpiece.

Straight bar: A somewhat stronger single bar bit is the straight bar. Pressure placed on the reins will press directly on the bars of the mouth. There is no room for the tongue to move away from the pressure to gain relief and there is very little flexibility. A straight bar bit might be a good option for horses that run through the rider's half halt, because it does give a fair amount of "whoa" to the horse that may be ignoring his rider.

Ported bits: As long as the reins are attached directly to the mouthpiece, the ported bit is still a snaffle, even though some people think a port on a single bar mouthpiece makes it a curb bit (see Myths and Misconceptions, page 128). In this case, the port actually serves to relieve the pressure of the bit on the tongue, rather than

This unique bit has a Segundo-style mouthpiece. It is a good bit for horses that need a little more than a snaffle, but don't quite need a leverage bit.

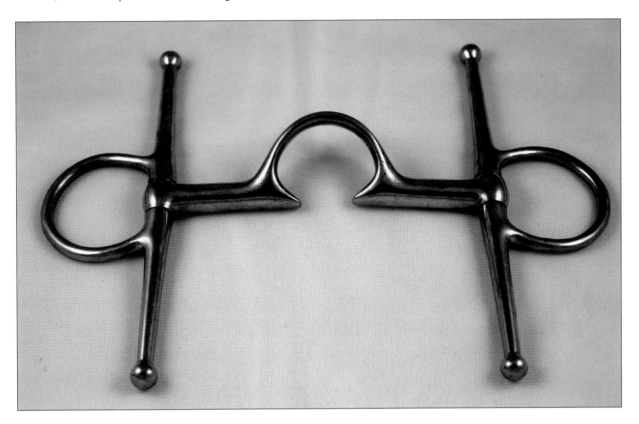

109

swiveling back and forth on its fulcrum with rein pressure, as in a leverage bit. Ports can be high, low, wide, or narrow.

While somewhat rare, ported loose ring, eggbutt, and other cheek piece snaffles do exist. Like all single-bar bits, ported bits lack the flexibility of a double- or single-jointed mouthpiece, but the port allows room for the tongue. They generally do not work well for horses that need additional work on jaw flexion and softness because they don't have much "play" in the mouth.

Ported snaffle bits are used by both English and Western riders when they are making the transition from a snaffle—direct contact—to a leverage bit, such as a curb

or a Weymouth. They can also be used for horses who dislike the rattle of the jointed bit in their mouths and prefer a steadier mouthpiece. Ported bits vary in severity primarily by the height of the port and the amount of tongue, bar, and lip pressure they apply when there is rein contact. A general rule of thumb is, the softer the arc of the metal, the gentler the bit. An arched "correction" bit with a flattened-out port and gently arched canons allows the tongue to rest in its natural position with little pressure when the reins are not engaged. Conversely, the Hanoverian bit has a high, deep port that could poke the palate, along with the straight

The ultra-flexible Waterford is excellent for horses that lean on the bit.

110

canons that press on the bars when too much pressure is applied.

Other Snaffle Mouthpieces

Waterford: This bit is used mostly in the hunter/jumper arena. It serves its purpose well—to encourage a horse that leans on the bit to carry himself. Most experts agree that a Waterford is a training bit, used temporarily to fix a problem. With just a series of links attached to the bit rings, this mouthpiece is really just a

somewhat softer version of a chain. It is so flexible it provides no support for the horse. The Waterford, like other snaffles, comes with various bit rings, and should be fit a size wider than a regular jointed snaffle to prevent lip pinching. Any sawing motion with the hands, no matter how light—even just squeezing the reins with the fists—is going to drag this bit back and forth across the horse's tongue and have an impact on the horse's mouth. Additionally, it is practically impossible to establish a steady contact in

The Magennis, or MacGuiness as it is sometimes called, provides a textured surface for the horse to play with. It needs to be used by educated hands. A rider who "saws" with his hands can do serious damage to the horse's tongue.

such a flexible bit, so it's not for dressage and rarely seen in Western circles. It is a worthwhile option for retraining jumpers, but should be used by an experienced rider with steady hands, and even then with caution.

Magennis: This bit (also known as the MacGuinness) is a single-jointed bit with rollers embedded in the mouth. The square shape of the mouthpiece is sharper on the tongue, and the rollers encourage salivation. It also prevents the horse from crossing his jaws. These bits have gone out of fashion so it's rare to find one in use. Like the Waterford, squeeze each hand alternately—"saw" on the reins and you'll be sawing a crevice in your horse's tongue.

Flute bit: Another interesting variation is the "windsucker," "whistle," or "flute" bit. It has a hollow core, making it light, and holes in the mouthpiece. Flute bits come in straight bar and single-linked versions. Leaving a whistle bit in a horse's mouth to prevent windsucking is an old wives' tale. Its real use, like bits made of unique materials such as sweet iron or copper, is to encourage a softer, wetter mouth. Despite its names, the flute bit has nothing to do with a horse's respiration. Horses are exclusively nose breathers, so putting holes in a mouthpiece would have no impact on a horse's ability to breathe.

LEVERAGE MOUTHPIECES

While leverage cheeks can be different shapes and sizes, the mouthpieces of leverage bits fall into the same categories as those of snaffles. The leverage action, however, means the mouthpieces apply pressure in slightly different ways.

We return now to a quick bit anatomy lesson. The snaffle has direct contact from the rider's hand to the rein through the bit ring and to the bit. Once that pressure is applied the horse feels it in different places on his head: tongue, bars, lips, palate, and poll (through the bridle).

The leverage cheeks add a new dimension to how the bit interacts with the horse's overall way of going and his head

111

Snaffle Bit Overview

In general, a thicker mouthpiece is softer than a thin one. This doesn't necessarily apply to all horses, since those with small mouths and low palates may find thick bits uncomfortable, and as such, more harsh.

A bit attached to a loose ring—with rings that can turn through the holes in the bit—has horizontal and vertical movement. The flexibility means a horse is able to play with the bit in his mouth. A gentle aid serves as a reminder, rather than a demand. Loose, flexible bits generally work well for asking young horses to accept the bit, and for many who are already trained. It's a great all-purpose, go-to option for most horses.

A single-jointed bit has a nutcracker effect on the jaw when both reins are pulled at the same time. In the right hands, however, single-jointed bits are perfectly fine, all-purpose bits.

A double-jointed bit is both flexible and soft. The sharper the edges in the plates or rings in the middle joint, the more severe the bit. Dr. Bristol and Dick Christian bits, for example, are one step more severe than a KK bit. The rotation of the bit and the contact of a sharper edge with the tongue when rein pressure is applied means that these bits are potential options for horses that are a little less responsive but by and large cooperative. They might be worth trying for the horse that's heavy in the hands.

Cheeks matter in the overall effect of the bit. Loose rings allow the mouthpiece to slide up and down. Full cheeks, D-rings, and eggbutts have no vertical play.

The looser the cheek, the more lateral mobility the horse's mouth has. Hinges or loose rings have more lateral mobility that a solidly welded cheek.

The looser and wider the bit ring, the more "warning" the horse will have and the longer it will take for him to feel the rider's hand signals. The rein slides on the ring before it engages.

Conversely, the more solidly attached and small the cheek, the quicker the horse feels the rein reaction. The horse receives an almost instant signal from a very small-ringed D-ring or full cheek.

Mouthpieces that have some arc, or "mullen," to them equalize the pressure over the top and sides of the tongue and against the bars.

A very straight, solid mouthpiece leaves little room for tongue relief. Pressure is consistent and can be quite harsh.

Photo by: Dusty Perin.

The Western rider engages the leverage more strongly to encourage a deeper flexing of the horse's poll. Note the angle of the shanks.

113

Photo by: www.istockphoto.com

Horses that work in a nose-out frame, such as barrel racers and working cow horses, use curved shanks.

in the bridle. Leverage bits are designed to encourage the horse to flex at the poll through the use of pressure on his chin. The mouth, as a general rule, is less engaged in the overall bit action than with a snaffle. Horses wearing leverage bits should already understand lateral and jaw flexion, because leverage bits—even those with hinged shanks, are not designed for this purpose.

Proper adjustment of the curb strap is vital to a leverage bit's effectiveness. Like proper mouthpiece fit, the curb strap's fit, as well as the material you choose, is part of the overall effect of the leverage bit. A too-loose curb strap negates or slows down the action of the bit. A too-tight strap can cause discomfort and makes the action of the bit quicker and sharper. A properly adjusted curb strap is flat with no twists, and has room for two fingers between the horse and the strap or chain.

Curb or leverage bits are a more severe option than a snaffle, due to the extra pressure on the poll, chin, and tongue, and the overall leverage action. They should be used by experienced riders and well-trained horses who understand the concept of self-carriage—whether English or Western.

A connector, sometimes called a delta, turns the two reins of a Pelham into a single rein.

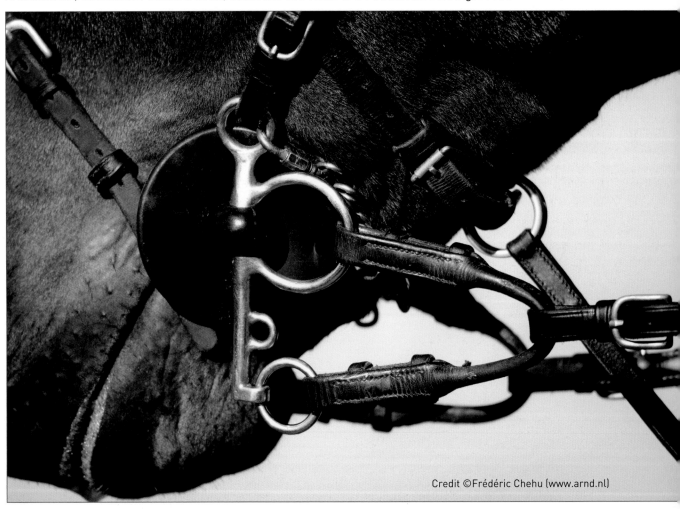

Credit ©Frédéric Chehu (www.arnd.nl)

As we discussed in chapter 9, there are two basic types of Western bit shanks—those that curve and those that are straight. Western mouthpieces range from single-jointed to high-ported spade bits. Whether the cheeks or shanks are fixed or swivel determines whether the rider can effectively use direct reining. Those "fixed cheeks" are for horses that already have developed some lateral flexibility. They don't need the encouragement of a direct rein to keep their jaw flexible. Fixed cheeks are welded onto the mouthpiece and do not move. Swivel cheeks or "loose jaw" cheeks have hinges. When the rider uses a direct rein, the shank or cheek moves to the side. It helps the horse to develop a softer jaw.

Horses that work in a nose-out, forward-going discipline, such as roping and barrel racing, are generally ridden in bits with curved shanks. The curve is both a function of tradition and also stays out of the way of the activity. Horses that are ridden in a rounder frame, with their noses perpendicular to the ground, tend to be ridden in straighter-shanked bits. This is quite similar to the English disciplines, where dressage horses with higher-level training wear straight-shanked leverage bits.

What follows is a brief description of some of the most popular leverage bit families.

English Leverage Bits

Pelhams

The Pelham bit has shanks of varying lengths. It has three or four rings on each shank, each serving a different purpose. The top ring attaches to the bridle. The largest ring (closest to the mouthpiece) attaches to the first set of reins, which, when used by itself, has no leverage. The next, little ring attaches to a lip strap, which is optional. The lower ring is for the second set of reins, which add the leverage action to the Pelham.

The rider using the Pelham bit has a couple of different options. He can hold both the snaffle and the curb rein in different hand configurations, depending on how much leverage he wants or needs on the bit; he can leave the curb rein soft, gathering it up only when necessary; or he can use both reins in a steadier contact. He can also attach a connector—called a delta or a rounding—between the two reins. This allows the rider to use just one pair of reins but engages both the snaffle and the leverage action. Roundings can be used with riders who are just learning to use curb bits, who don't know how, or don't want to bother with two pairs of reins. The curb strap of the Pelham should have two fingers' width between the chain and the chin.

Pelhams can come with linked or single-bar mouthpieces. Several common styles are described below.

Hartwell: The most common variety is a single bar with a small port, called a Hartwell or ported mouth. This bit has a small port that allows room for the tongue. Although Pelhams generally have swivel shanks, there is very little lateral action in a straight bar Pelham. When the rider engages the curb rein, it simultaneously swivels the port onto the tongue while engaging poll pressure. It also presses on the bars of the mouth.

115

Port-mouth Pelhams are very popular in the jumper and hunter rings, because they allow the rider to achieve both a modicum of "whoa" and balance while maintaining a properly flexed poll and head position.

Rubber mullen mouth Pelham: Like the mullen mouth snaffle, this is one of the gentlest forms of this bit. It allows plenty of soft flexibility while still engaging the leverage action. The pressure on the bars is still active, but is very soft. This is a good transition bit for the rider just learning to use a Pelham style bit, because even with its leverage action, the rubber mouth makes it very benign and forgiving. It is not recommended for those who need the power of bar pressure to control an overly exuberant horse. Tightening the reins brings the edges of the bit slightly closer together, which lightly loosens the curb strap, making it a little ineffective.

Arch-mouth Pelham: This mouthpiece is made of metal and has a mullen-like arc. It gives the rider a bit more control than the rubber version because the bar and tongue pressure comes from a solid metal. It's a good step up from a mullen mouth, but is not quite as potentially severe as the Hartwell.

Single-link Pelhams: These bits have recently become more popular (see Myths and Misconceptions, page 128). These mouthpieces aren't a good option for riders who don't understand the concept of pressure and release. Sustained pressure placed on the bars and the lower jaw results in a "nutcracker" of the canons of the bit. If you apply that concept to the Pelham style, there's an additional drawback: As the canons are drawn together by rein pressure, it actually *loosens* the curb strap or chain. If the chain is too loose, it loses its effectiveness overall and can become an irritant to the horse, dangling against his chin. The rider has to pull much harder to achieve any type of pressure, which of course increases the pressure on tongue

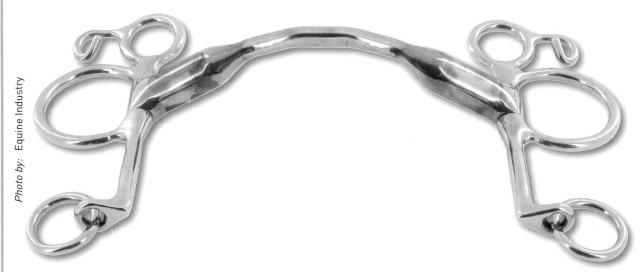

Photo by: Equine Industry

The arc of this Pelham allows room for the tongue. It also has short shanks, so the leverage is very light.

116

Photo by: Equine Industry

On this short-shanked Pelham, the single link mouthpiece works like a single-jointed snaffle when the snaffle rein is engaged.

and bars as well as the potential of the joint poking into the roof of the mouth.

Another key problem with the linked Pelham is that it is a misconstrued hybrid: with a flexible mouthpiece on a bit designed to be used in a curb style, it offers neither the encouragement to flex the jaw nor the leverage action of the engaged curb strap. And contrary to popular belief, a jointed Pelham is not a "beginner's" Pelham, because of the enhanced nutcracker effect when the leverage rein is engaged. Using a Pelham with a jointed bit requires a very well schooled horse who needs little rein pressure to respond.

Hanoverian: This mouthpiece on a Pelham is an older style bit, used primarily in the U.K. and mostly for polo ponies, jumpers, and other excitable types of horses. It has a very high port that's jointed, which allows some independent control of either side of the horse's mouth. The Hanoverian Pelham is quite a strong bit, because engaging the leverage rein applies a lot of pressure on the bars and the tongue. It's a bit similar to the Western spade bit in that it rests lightly until needed, and then is quite strong.

Double-linked, French link, and Dr. Bristol: These Pelhams offer the flexibility and softness of these mouthpieces, but not very much leverage. Because these bits have so much movement, engaging the leverage rein loosens the curb chain, but adds just a little bit of added pressure on the bars.

New mouthpieces: New innovations in Pelham bit mouthpieces include the Happy Mouth, with its signature wavy mouthpiece; the Dynamic from Sprenger, which features the company's angled lozenge in the center of a double-linked mouthpiece; and the Myler, with its signature barrel and arced mouthpiece that curves over the tongue. Mikmar has created its own version of the Pelham, with a very wide mouthpiece made

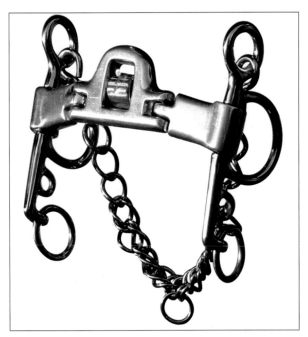

A jointed Pelham from Mikmar. The wide, light-weight mouthpiece covers more tongue area than the other Pelhams.

of lightweight alloy, a copper roller, and a slanted-back port to rest on tongue.

Kimberwicke

The D-ring, non-slotted, single-jointed Kimberwicke mouthpiece differs very little from a D-ring snaffle except for one important point: the Kimberwicke has a curb strap and rectangular bridle rings. The shape and location of the bridle rings add a little more leverage than a simple D-ring. An Uxeter Kimberwicke, which has slots for reins, together with a single jointed mouthpiece is more effective, but for the real results of a Kimberwicke, an Uxeter with a ported single-bar mouthpiece is the most effective of this style of bit.

Mullen mouth, ported, and Hanoverian mouthpieces are all available with Kimberwicke cheek pieces.

Weymouth (Double Bridle)

For most readers, this section won't be particularly useful. The double bridle is now almost exclusively used on upper-level dressage horses and for some park horses, such as Tennessee Walkers and Saddlebreds. In a way, it's very similar to how a spade bit

Photo by: Equine Industry.

The baby Pelham Dr. Bristol is two bits in one: a Dr. Bristol snaffle, and a jointed Pelham, depending on which set of reins is engaged.

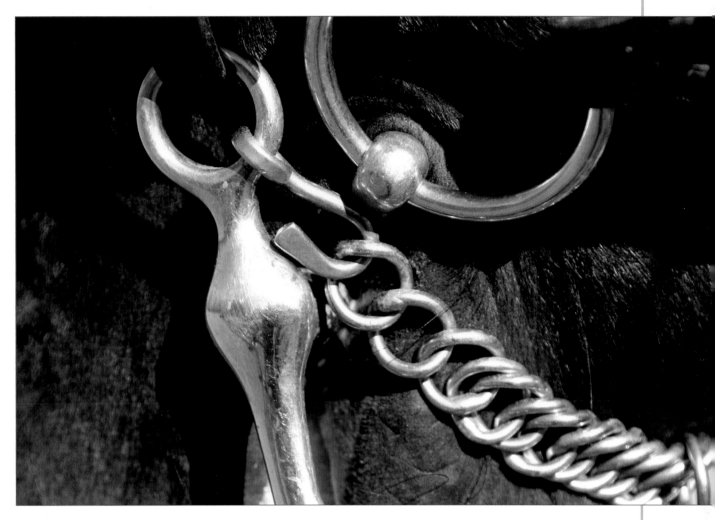

The fit of the double-bridle is very important. The snaffle bit sits above the curb, with the chain flat and between the two.

is used in Western riding, which is only after the horse has reached a very high level of training.

Double bridles consist of a Weymouth curb bit and a bradoon (or bridoon) snaffle with small loose rings. The Weymouth is very similar to a bar-mouth or ported Pelham, only it's built to be used in a double bridle. The bradoon is similar to a loose ring snaffle, only it, too, is designed to be used with the double bridle. The mouthpieces can vary in width, depending on the size of the horse's mouth and his preferences.

Most importantly, the Weymouth must fit correctly, with very little space between the bit cheek and horse's cheek. Riders who use double bridles commonly prefer a thinner, low-ported curb bit and a single or double-jointed bradoon in combination.

Just as in Western bitting, the length of the cheek pieces and the tightness of the curb chain on the Weymouth will determine the amount of leverage. The snaffle bit sits in the horse's mouth above the curb bit, allowing enough space for it to be used on its own, but not so high in the mouth that it risks rubbing the molars or pinching the cheeks. It's also preferable to use thinner versions of both the snaffle and the curb bit.

Both bits should be snug against the horse's lips to prevent chafing. Many double bridle users put some Vaseline or other lubricant on their horse's lips.

Elwyn Hartley Edwards[14] quotes a well-known horseman as saying the double bridle has an "up and in" effect. The leverage serves to bring flexion to the horse's poll while the pressure on the curb strap encourages him to keep his nose in rather than poked out. The tighter the curb, the quicker the bit comes into action.

The double bridle has been around since the sixteenth century, but its use is widely misunderstood. Even in today's dressage arenas, there are plenty of riders, especially since a recent rule change allows the use of the double bridle at third level dressage, who have no business riding in one. A double bridle adds finesse to the solidly trained basics for an advanced rider and well-trained horse.

So why bother with the extra bit? For one, Pelhams are generally not allowed in dressage competition. The addition of the snaffle allows the rider to maintain the soft and steady contact necessary for a horse

The curb shouldn't be too wide. It should fit relatively snugly against the horse's mouth. This curb doesn't fit very well.

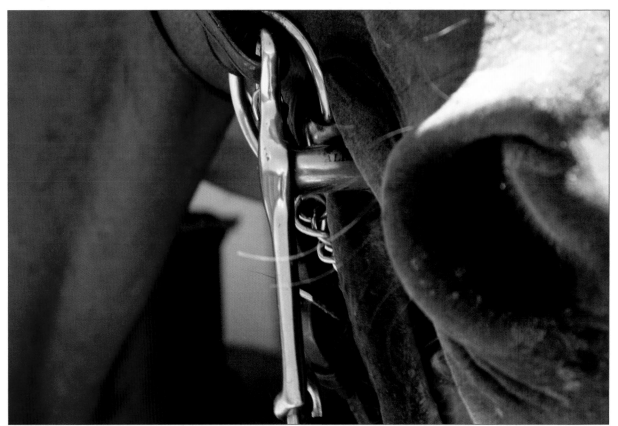

working at the upper levels of dressage. The well-trained horse will respond to the rider's signals through a gentle hand on the snaffle.

The curb, on the other hand, can encourage the horse to flex his poll. It should not be used to *position* the horse's poll, although that's what many people think. At this stage of training, the horse should carry himself, with a strong topline, bending hocks, and gently flexed head perpendicular to the ground. The addition of the curb can encourage the horse to be more flexible, but it does not create that flexibility.

When the double bridle is used, a well-schooled rider will spend most of his time using the bradoon. That rein will appear steadily connected to the horse's mouth, while the curb rein will be employed very judiciously with only a squeeze or a gentle twist of the wrist.

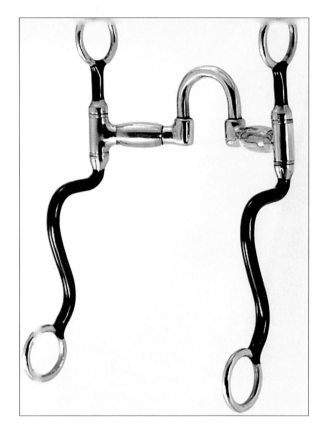

A high-ported correction mouthpiece allows room for the horse's tongue. This version has long shanks but is jointed, which allows some lateral flexibility.

WESTERN CURB OR LEVERAGE BITS

Correction Mouthpiece

A high-ported mouthpiece that allows room for the tongue, a correction mouthpiece is usually found with leverage shanks of varying lengths. The correction bit has good stopping power and can be used for horses that need a little extra help to rate their rhythm correctly. The port is high enough that it can touch the roof of the horse's mouth, so this bit should be used with caution. It also sometimes has a "cricket" or copper roller in the middle.

Tom Thumb

A single-jointed mouthpiece on a shorter leverage shank, this bit has a very strong action (see Myths and Misconceptions, page 156). It has both the nutcracker effect of the single-jointed mouthpiece and the leverage of a curb bit, which means it can squeeze the lower jaw between the shanks. This bit should be used by experienced hands.

Argentine

A bit similar to the English-style Pelham, the Argentine bit has a snaffle ring and a shorter-shanked curb ring. It generally has a single-link mouthpiece, which, when used

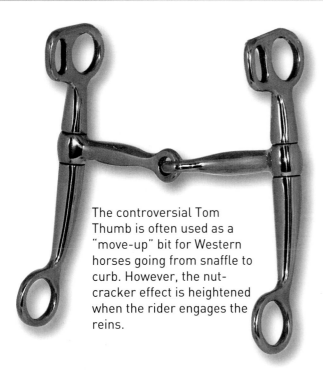

The controversial Tom Thumb is often used as a "move-up" bit for Western horses going from snaffle to curb. However, the nut-cracker effect is heightened when the rider engages the reins.

Spoon Mouth or Cathedral Mouth

Both of these options have a rather high port but are flattened instead of round. Some have a roller in the middle to encourage tongue play. This is a very strong bit with the potential for harming the roof of the horse's mouth. It is for the finished bridle horse and the experienced rider.

Thumb Port

This is a flattened, high port that's wider than a spoon port. It often comes with a copper roller in the middle and linked, rather

with the curb rein alone, makes it similar to the Tom Thumb. But when used in combination with a pair of reins attached to the snaffle ring, it can be a good bit for converting from snaffle to curb. Use a delta or a converter to turn the two pairs of reins into one.

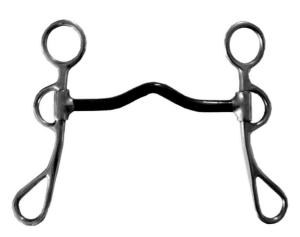

The Argentine bit has a snaffle rein as well as a curb rein. This is a much better option for moving up the Western training scale than the Tom Thumb.

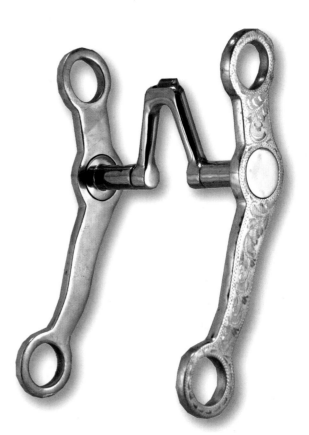

The high-ported cathedral bit allows room for the tongue. Many have rounded instead of flattened ports. Its high port can make contact with the roof of the mouth, so it is for experienced hands on well-trained horses.

than solid connections to the canons. This is a good bit for the very well-trained bridle horse that needs a little encouragement to loosen his jaw.

Billy Allen

A jointed mouthpiece covered with a barrel, the Billy Allen is a hybrid between the link bit and a solid-mouthed bit. Most Billy Allens come with a snaffle ring and a shank allowing reining multiple options. It's a good bit for transitioning from the snaffle to the curb.

Spade Bit

Like the double bridle for dressage, the spade bit is for the highly trained horse and rider pair. Generally, a spade bit is a combination of several elements: a high port angled toward the back of the throat, made of a spoon, cricket, and copper-covered braces. The horse is trained to pick up the bit, rather than respond to its pressure. The angle of the spoon prevents the port from poking the roof of the horse's mouth.

Your spade bit could have a high leverage action or a low leverage action. It depends on where the mouthpiece is placed in relationship to the shanks—higher up or lower down.

The spade bit has many components that have an impact on its action. The cheek pieces on some spade bits swivel. Like mouthpieces on other curb bits, the spade can come with a softer mouthpiece that curves against the bars, or a straighter mouthpiece that has more pressure on the

bars. Spade bits, and horses properly trained to wear them, are both works of art.

Leverage Bit Overview

1) Leverage bits are for riders who understand the impact of these bits on a horse's mouth and head, or riders under supervision of a trainer. A leverage bit with a snaffle rein makes a good starter leverage bit or one for a horse that gets overly exuberant doing certain activities. The rider can engage the leverage when needed and leave it slack when things are fine. For English riders, changing to a thinner snaffle or one with a different shape may be just as effective as putting a leverage bit in a horse's mouth.

2) The longer the shank, the more pounds per square millimeter of pressure will be engaged when the rider takes up the reins.

3) Leverage bits are not a substitute for good training, but can be used to reinforce a training lesson ("wait, balance, pay attention to my seat, drop your poll, flex more"). In the Western arena, leverage or curb bits should be used only after the horse and rider have been well trained to neck rein, with the rider understanding the proper engagement of leverage with the timing of his aids and correct use of the reins.

4) A single-jointed mouthpiece on a leverage-style bit does not make it softer than a bar mouthpiece. Instead, it may be one of the most uncomfortable bits we've invented. The combination of the jointed action of the mouthpiece and the leverage action of the shanks exacerbates

123

the nutcracker effect, basically strangling the jaw. A bit like this must be used with a great deal of care.

5) If you are moving from a snaffle to a curb, consider a loose-jawed, short shank, open-ported bit to give the horse plenty of room for his tongue and only a gentle curb action.

6) The wider the port, the less tongue pressure there is.

7) The steeper the port, the more likely it will be to make contact with the sensitive upper palate. It takes about two inches of port in a normal horse to make contact with the roof of the mouth.

8) To determine the amount of leverage, consider the length and shape of the shank. The amount of angle; whether straight, grazing, 7-shaped, or S-shaped; and the length of each part of the shank and the ratio of the two determines the leverage and quickness. For example, a short purchase and a long shank is a very quick and highly leveraged bit. The greater the ratio, the quicker the bit, and the more leverage it has.

GAGS

This unique family of bits should only be used by experienced riders and trainers, or under the supervision of a trainer, because in the wrong hands they can be quite severe.

The action of the gag differs from the curb in several significant ways:

- There's no curb strap. That means that when the rider pulls on the reins,

there's no corresponding pressure on the chin groove to ask the horse to give at the poll. There is, however, some poll pressure.

- The gag bit applies much more pressure on the lips than on the tongue or the bars. While some gags do have a rein that goes over the poll, this isn't their first point of action.

- The gag bit, according to Elwyn Hartley Edwards, has a "both ends against the middle" action: The pressure on the mouth is upwards, while the pressure on the poll is downward.

- Gags can be fit with a snaffle rein as well, so the rider can employ the gag when necessary but use mostly the snaffle.

Conventional Gag Bit

A conventional gag bit has rope or rounded leather pieces (roundings) that attach to the crown pieces of your bridle. The roundings slide through the gag bit rings quickly and allow you to release the gag action in an instant.

The conventional gag bit generally has D or Eggbutt bit rings (in fact, in the U.K. it is called a "gag snaffle"), through which you can also attach a direct rein. The gag rein goes through both sides of the bit ring, attaching to the bridle rings on both cheeks and to the regular reins. The pressure on the reins does not get diffused through the length of the shank—it goes directly to the horse's poll, one of his most sensitive parts. The gag, when engaged, lifts up against the horse's lips.

The gag bit is used in the English disciplines almost exclusively for jumping and for polo. It is frequently seen on the cross-country course and in the stadium-jumping arena. Its particular action works very well for rebalancing a horse that may be running flat on his forehand. The rider in this case can take a hold of the gag rein and, using seat and leg simultaneously, rebalance the horse before the jump. The gag bit asks the horse to lift his head and allows the rider to bring a horse that may be curled up with his head between his knees up in front.

The gag bit is illegal in the dressage arena and is never seen in the hunter ring. It is assumed that there is no reason for a hunter to need a gag, since he's supposed to have a quiet, rated, and gentle way of going. Sometimes a gag bit may be used temporarily as a training device to correct a horse that's too low in the poll and/or too strong.

Photo by: © Jacques Toffi/www.arnd.nl

Gags are popular with polo players and jumper riders. It allows them to bring their horses' heads up quickly.

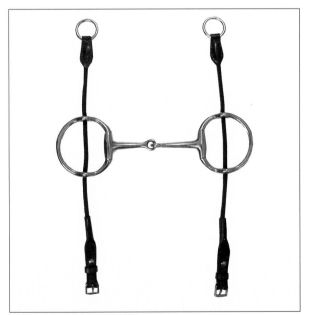

The conventional gag is designed to have both a snaffle and a gag rein. It is sometimes called a gag snaffle.

There are several varieties of gags, with all varieties of mouthpieces. There are single-jointed, double-jointed, twisted wire, mullen mouth, French link, cherry roller, and everything in between.

Wonder Gag

The wonder gag slides up in the horse's mouth and applies pressure to the lips when the reins are engaged. It often has a very thin mouthpiece, and wide rings that allow the snaffle rein to slide. The lower shanks can be used when the rider needs both more leverage and more gag action. It is often seen in the Western arena as well.

The thin mouthpiece and multiple ways to attach the reins make this wonder gag a particularly versatile bit for the strong, forward-going horse. It is for experienced riders only.

126

Elevator Bits

There is very little difference between an "elevator" and a "gag" bit. A traditional gag has cheek rings and roundings, while an elevator may have shanks that look more like a curb or other leverage bit. Both are designed to lift in the horse's mouth before the leverage action engages.

With the traditional gag, the mouthpiece itself slides on the rein rings, giving the horse an "upward" signal, hence the term "elevator."

Both gag and elevator bits give the horse some "warning" before their full effect is engaged. The first action the horse feels is the bit sliding up the rings as the rider takes more contact. The bit lifts in the mouth. The second action is the engagement of the leverage on the poll. Because there is no curb strap on the elevator or gag bits, the cheek pieces of the bridle are pulled forward and down when the rein is engaged.

Because the action of the bit is upward, the lips are the primary point of engagement for the linked variety of mouthpieces. The bit might actually draw up toward the back of the horse's throat and against his molars should the rider need serious pull.

The so-called American gag's shanks add a leverage component, although there is no curb strap preventing the bit from rising up against the lips when the rider pulls on the reins.

Dutch Gag

The Dutch gag is also called a Pessoa, a European, a Continental, a four-ring, or a bubble bit. What differentiates it from a traditional gag is the multiple leverage options available to riders. This style of bit has recently come into favor among jumper riders. The bits have two, three, or four rings of differing widths. This allows the rider to choose the ring he needs for that day's ride. The smaller rings give the horse less warning, while the bigger ring at the bit allows the rein to slide up before engaging the mouth pressure and leverage on the poll. The lowest ring is the smallest, the furthest from the mouthpiece, and the most severe. The lack of curb strap or chain means the bit moves up in the mouth and applies lip pressure, while also adding additional poll pressure intensity. Because of the amount of play in the lowest ring, and the mouthpiece's flexibility, this bit can both bring the head up and provide the action of a relatively strong leverage bit.

THE BITLESS BRIDLES

There are many different kinds of bitless bridles, and it seems new ones are being invented every day. As with bits, there are families of bitless bridles that share characteristics and work well with certain kinds of horses or training problems. Bridles

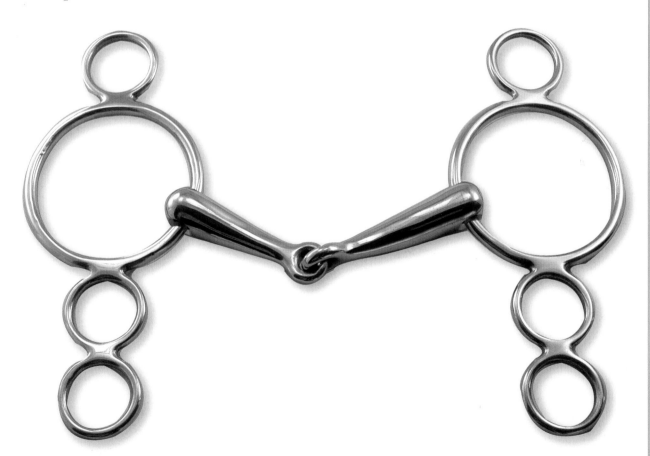

The Dutch gag allows the rider to adjust the leverage. The rings provide a bit of "signal" to the horse before action is engaged.

127

without mouthpieces, bitless bridles, also called nose bridles, work like regular bridles and bits, only they use pressure points on the head rather than in the mouth.

That pressure is employed in a couple of ways. First there are the shanked versions, which employ leverage. There are rope hackamores that use texture and rein pressure. And there is a relatively new family of bitless bridles that use nose, cheek, and overall head pressure to direct the horse.

Western Hackamore

The bitless bridle has a very long history, based on the Spanish conquistadors' training methods of starting horses in rope halters and gradually moving them, as training allowed, into the spade bit of finished bridle horse. Early European settlers brought those methods to California.

The word "hackamore" actually originates from the Spanish *jaquima*, meaning halter or headstall. It may have originally been brought to Spain by the Moors, who used a "hackma"—a rope halter, basically—to control camels. The word "hackamore" is often interchanged with "bosal," used to describe a rope bridle without a bit. However, a bosal is actually just the noseband of a hackamore, not the entire structure.

The vaquero horse's progression from hackamore to snaffle to curb to spade bit underscores the importance to the vaqueros of proper training—lightness in the bridle came only after the horse had been properly trained to the seat and leg. Another theory as to why the hackamore was the tack of choice for the young horse in the Spanish tradition

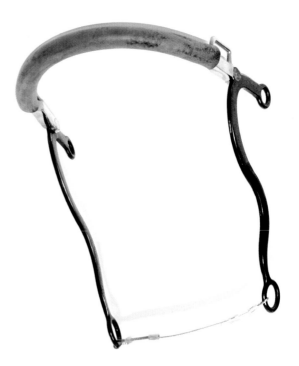

This hackamore has a rubber-covered metal noseband and long shanks. The hobble keeps the shanks from splaying apart.

had to do with the horse's maturity. A young horse doesn't have his full set of adult teeth until he's four or older. The teeth directly adjacent to the bars tend to be the last to grow in. A horse that's already sensitive in the mouth doesn't need the added irritation of a piece of metal.

The classic bosal hackamore has a low noseband and a rope knot to which is tied the throatlatch, or *fiador*. The word "fiador" can also refer to the large knot where the reins and an additional long rope are attached to the noseband.

Robert Miller, DVM, the noted equine behaviorist, draws the similarity between the vaquero method of starting horses in the bosal hackamore and today's "natural" horsemanship clinicians, who nearly all work with horses in a rope halter with knots at the pressure points. The hackamore has a thicker noseband and a fiador knot, but beyond that, it isn't much different from a rope halter. It also very much proves the theory that you don't need a bit for control. Anyone who's ever been truly run away with knows just how little a bit really does in stopping a panicked horse. As such, a bit is a communication tool rather than a control device, and a bitless bridle, a rope halter, or a Western hackamore are all just as effective at communication.

The rope hackamore has multiple parts that signal the horse. It has the noseband—the actual bosal—which is generally made of braided rawhide over a twisted rawhide

With its thick, low-set noseband and heavy fiador, the bosal hackamore teaches the horse to yield to pressure on his nose.

core. It is attached to the fiador, which forms the throatlatch, and the mecate (a long rein) through a heel knot. The bosal is positioned slightly lower on the nose than a regular cavesson noseband.

Proper placement of any type of hackamore is crucial—the bosal must sit just under the nasal bone where the cartilage begins. A misplaced hackamore noseband can squeeze the horse's nose. These are extremely delicate structures that can be easily damaged, so make sure that any rein pressure is quick and gentle—pressure, release. Otherwise you can make your horse want to evade, causing many adverse and resistant behaviors.

A secondary aspect that makes a Western rope hackamore an excellent training bridle is the way riders use it to direct the horse's nose. The bosal, which is stiff, applies pressure, but the movement of the hand and arm out to the side and the pressure on the mecate rein also serve as a visual guide for the greener horse.

Rope Halter

The decision to include a rope halter in a book about bits and in a section on bitless bridles was tough. After all, it isn't really a bridle. Yet, there are so many trainers using rope halters today in much the way the vaqueros and Spanish traditional riders use the hackamore that it's worth a brief explanation and inclusion.

The rope halter's main attribute is that it has strategically placed knots that apply pressure to the horse's face. The horse learns to move away from the pressure using a

129

combination of body language and rope signals. You can tie two mecate-type lead ropes to the bottom of the loop to use as reins, and as you use them, the knots on the halter apply pressure on his face. While it is not a very refined way to ride, it is very effective for young horses, building trust in both horse and rider, and developing the type of partnership that enhances the horse-human relationship. Most horses that start in a rope halter eventually graduate to a snaffle bit.

MECHANICAL HACKAMORE OR HACKAMORE BIT

Mechanical hackamores are constructed similarly to leverage bits, with a curb chain or strap, shanks of varying lengths, and a solid, often rigid piece that fits over the nose. The pressure that's created from the rider's contact with the reins presses the noseband against the horse's nose and pulls the bridle cheek pieces downward, applying pressure on his poll. Mechanical hackamores, like all leverage bits, can be quite harsh in the wrong hands. In fact, a misused mechanical hackamore can break a horse's nose.

As with all leverage bits, the length of the shanks determines the ratio of rider contact to the pressure on the poll, chin groove, and the nose. Shanks can be long or short, straight or S-shaped. Mechanical hackamores

A rope halter uses pressure from the knots to teach the horse to yield.

have very little lateral action. Their primary use is vertical flexion of the head and poll.

As with mouthpieces, the theory of "thicker equals softer" applies. Note the use of the word "theory"—sometimes it's true, but sometimes horses prefer something different. So, the wider the noseband on the mechanical hackamore, the less severe it is. You also have to take into consideration the length and shape of the shanks.

In chapter 3, we discussed the sensitivity of the horse's nose and chin grooves. The hackamore plays directly on these sensitivities. There are several kinds of hackamore nosebands, and like bits, they range from mild to severe. The shanks can also be different shapes—straight, S-curved, angled back, or 7-shaped. As with the leverage shanks, the more angled the shank, the milder the impact.

Hackamore Nosebands

Rubber covered chain nose: The rubber softens the impact of the chain, but the flexibility and thinness of the noseband mean it can be quite strong.

Rope or braided leather nosebands: These tend to be thin and flexible, and as such, provide a fair amount of "rate"—ability to bring the horse to the rhythm in which you'd like him to travel.

Flat leather noseband: This hackamore is one of the most popular styles for both English and Western. It's good for horses that carry themselves and are well tuned to the rider, because their action is quite mild.

131

Sidepulls, Dr. Cook Bridles, and LG Bridles

The third category of bitless bridle puts pressure on the horse's head. The cross-under bitless bridle, invented by Robert Cook, DVM, works on the principle of pressure and release. The cross-under's most distinguishing feature is the unique configuration of the throatlatch. Rather than a single strap, the cross-under has two throatlatches, which cross below the horse's jaw and attach to the reins. When the rider takes contact, the horse feels it on the opposite cheek and poll. Cook claims the real difference is that the horse feels a "push" or a "nudge" rather than the pull of the traditional bridle and rein combination. The nudge effect is secondary to the aids of good riding—seat, leg, and weight. The bridle is designed to disperse the pressure from the rider's aids to a variety of areas rather than localizing it to the most sensitive areas of the horse's mouth.

One potential drawback for the cross-under is that riders with unsteady contact tend to cause the horse's head to wag. Because the release happens when the leather reins slide through the rings, which subsequently loosens the throatlatches, it can also take a split second longer to release the contact than in a snaffle bit. The bridle also needs to be well oiled to facilitate the release.

Cook's research showed how the horses in a riding school program reacted to the cross-under bitless bridle. When four different horses were ridden through a basic training level dressage test twice, once in a regular snaffle bit and once in a bitless bridle of Cook's design, the average score increased significantly and the horses were softer and less fussy.

The results aren't surprising. It is the nature of school horses' jobs that their mouths are often yanked on, pulled on, and balanced on during their lessons, and hence they are as a general rule defensive, no matter what's in their mouths. Using the cross-under bridle steadied the contact and gave the school horses significant relief.

Another bitless design is the LG Bridle. Invented by Monica Lehmenkühler, of Cologne, Germany, the bridle works differently from the Cook bridle in a number of ways. The LG consists of two wheels, a soft leather noseband, and a curb chain, which is attached to the noseband with leather loops. It can be strapped to any regular bridle. The adjustment of the reins, bridle cheek pieces, and curb chain determine whether there is more or less leverage. With tension on the reins, the wheel turns, shortening the noseband, curb chain, and finally the crownpiece of the bridle. This product works like a mechanical hackamore, employing a very light amount of leverage, or it can put more direct pressure on the nose, depending on the adjustment.

While Western riders have been using rope hackamores and other bitless options forever, the number of new

133

Dr. Robert Cook's bridle's throatlatch crosses under the chin. Horses feel the rein pressure as a push from the opposite side, rather than a direct pull.

inventions geared toward the English riding market might signal that bitless bridles are no longer a "fad" but have actually become relatively accepted by the mainstream horse community. While you may see a bitless bridle in the hunt field, on the trail, or even

134

The LG Bridle, invented in Germany, uses a wheel at each cheek. The reins can be adjusted in different places along the wheels for direct or leverage pressure on the nose and poll.

in the arena, they are illegal in recognized dressage competitions and not used in the hunter show ring.

The bitless options seem particularly useful for riding schools, as Cook notes. Teaching inexperienced riders that bits are not brakes, and that it's possible to both steer and stop without pulling on the horse's mouth, would do much to further equestrian education.

Any horse in any discipline can be ridden in a bitless bridle provided he's well trained.

Country
Mortgages

Photo by: John Brasseaux

CHAPTER - 11

WHICH BIT AND WHY?

Dr. Cook is perhaps correct when he says that traditional bitting and bridles are based on pain avoidance as a means of training. In the early days of horsemanship, that's all our ancestors knew. As we learned more about horses and our relationship with them has evolved, however, we have begun to understand training principles that use communication and cooperation as a means to train our horses.

The word "submission" is used liberally in horse training circles. Yet do we want submission? Or do we prefer partnership? When you watch a highly trained horse and rider team in the reining, cutting, dressage, or jumper rings, the rider appears only to be breathing his commands. The hands stay low, the body signals gently, the horse performs. It's seamless and beautiful and embodies the goal to which many horse people aspire. And yet, we're always looking for the toy or the tool or the item that will be the key to our horse's mouth, as that nineteenth-century loriner Latchford described. In reality, we may not be looking for the single key, but rather for the combination of training, proper aids, and bit, bridle, and noseband that will make our horses most cooperative and happy to go along with our commands.

The rise of the natural horsemanship phenomenon has perhaps brought this idea of partnership even more to the forefront. Gone are the days when a strong bit was considered the answer to a strong horse. Thanks to individuals like Tom Dorrance, Ray Hunt, Pat Parelli, and John Lyons, their disciples, and the popularity of "natural" trainers (there are too many to name here,) we're now much more aware of the value of gentle training methods to coax our horses into calmness and cooperation.

At the top of any equestrian sport, the goal is softness and submission.

Nonetheless there are still plenty of reasons to evaluate your horse's bit and to make sure he's in the one that makes him most comfortable. If you become an expert at reading your horse's signals, it becomes easier to determine what's going on with your horse.

As we noted, symptoms of bit discomfort are often misdiagnosed. Sometimes it manifests in head tossing, bucking, getting strong in the bridle, pulling, or running away (in extreme cases). More mild symptoms of discomfort include opening and closing the mouth, poking the nose out, or grabbing the bit between the teeth and hanging on

it. Other horses may grind their teeth, put their tongue over the bit, or stick it out the side (see page 120). A happy horse should carry the bit in his mouth gently. He should be light and soft, so he responds instantly to a gentle close of the fist or slight shift in position of the hand.

There's no real way to know what bit is right for your horse. You can try as many bits as there are stars in the sky and still not come up with a solution. That's because bitting is a whole horse issue, not a mouth issue.

So before you buy out your local tack store looking for the key to your horse's happiness, consider the following:

137

Photo by: Dusty Perin

138

Physical discomfort is easy to spot if you know what to look for. Head tossing, bucking, and resistance to the aids are all signs of an unhappy horse.

1) **The horse's training.** The most crucial element of bitting is the proper training of the horse for your particular discipline. He absolutely must understand the relationship between the seat, the legs, and the hands in order to properly accept the bit. Every riding discipline has its own training pyramid, and at the base of all of them is rhythm. A horse that speeds up, slows down, and/or is otherwise inconsistent in his gaits has not accepted his rider's aids. Suppleness and softness are also fundamental no matter the discipline. As 2009 World Cup dressage winner Steffen Peters says, there are three important things to work on: Suppleness, suppleness, and suppleness. If the horse is tense, he's not able to maintain a rhythm, his back muscles are stiff, and that stiffness will travel up his neck and head into his mouth.

2) **Your discipline.** As you'll see in the case studies below, horses sometimes have trouble moving from one discipline to

another, because the concept of contact might be different. This is especially true of horses that go from being well-trained Western horses to either dressage or hunter/jumpers, where riders prefer to have a soft but steady contact with the bit. The horse who's been trained to be light in the bridle and let the bit just hang gently in his mouth and is suddenly confronted with what feels to him like hard hands may respond by grabbing the bit or running from the contact. The opposite is also true—a horse used to steady contact in a snaffle-type bit may be quite surprised and confused by a curb bit with a port.

3) **Your riding ability.** Are you able to post the trot without your hands following you? Do you know the meaning of independent aids? More often than not, mouth problems can be traced back to the rider's own incompetence. Master Nuño Oliveira, the great equestrian and author of the great work *Reflections on Equestrian Art*, writes, "Only a rider with a proper position can obtain valid results from his horse." Without a secure seat, a strong midsection, and relaxed and non-pinching legs, it will be nearly impossible for a rider to carry his hands quietly no matter what the horse is doing. This takes work. It takes training, and it takes plenty of hours in the saddle. To be a truly great athlete also means taking some measures to be fit off the horse. The poorly ridden horse can, according to Dr. Cook's research, develop thicker membranes over the gums and spurs on the bones of the bars. Any horse, improperly trained and ridden, is going to develop a hard mouth or other bad habits that may make him ultimately fall into the "bad horse" category. It isn't his fault, by and large, but ours. To achieve softness of the mouth, we have to strive to become riders that practice "equilibrium in motion" and can maintain our seats and balance without using our hands, and train our horses to cooperate with the slightest signal from the rider.

4) **A thorough understanding of the theory of bitting.** Changing a cheek ring may make as much difference as switching from a single to a double-jointed bit. There's no exact recipe for success, but knowing how each part works and how the variations have an impact on the overall apparatus can at least give most thinking horsemen a baseline knowledge from which to start their bitting experimentation.

There are many, many variables and factors to take into consideration when choosing a bit. And like a veterinarian trying to diagnose an elusive illness, we only have the horse's reactions to guide us to our choices. No matter how you apply the above guidelines, the horse should be the one to tell you what works for him.

Finding the right bit is a matter of patience and observation. Begin your bit journey by first determining why you want to change bits in the first place. If your horse is moving well, cooperating, and going in a nice, relaxed manner, perhaps there's no

139

reason to change bits at all. As the old saw goes, "if it ain't broke, don't fix it."

A trainer's suggestion that you change bits isn't a good reason. You have to question why the trainer thinks it's necessary, and ask for a thorough explanation. It may be possible that the trainer sees something from the ground that you're not feeling in the saddle.

Trying a new bit should be justified—it should be the result of a problem that has cropped up and for which you are working on a training solution. Consider how a doctor diagnoses a medical issue. First he'll take your vital signs. He'll interview you about your symptoms. Then he'll make a diagnosis and prescribe medication. If the medication doesn't work, he'll bring you back to the office for another series of tests or he may just try a different medication.

That's how your bit problem-solving attempts should go. Begin by taking your horse's training vital signs: Is he soft and supple in the bridle? Is he carrying his head properly? Is his body in good shape? How does his tack fit? Is his neck straight when he's traveling forward? Is his head tilted or cocked one way or the other?

Then do a thorough examination of his mouth for sore spots or abrasions. Note the location of the sores (if they exist). This is key to figuring out what's gone awry with your training program and how to fix it. For example, a horse that leans on the bridle when you're going left but not when you're going right might be crooked or have a sore leg. A rider with uneven hands may cause a rub mark on one lip but not on the other.

From this set of observations, you can then determine whether your bitting problem is a rider-caused issue that can be solved with training, a physical problem that requires a veterinarian's help, or a true bitting problem.

Before you make any changes to the horse's bit, step back and retrain the foundation. Work the horse in a rhythm from your seat and leg. Ride your horse from his hindquarters, not from his bridle. Seek the help of a professional.

After you've evaluated your riding and your horse's training, then it might be time to change bits. You can do this concurrently with training, but to go back to our medical example, it doesn't help the diagnosis to be trying two prescriptions at once to see which one works. It might be that you'll develop an exercise to help the horse while trying a new bit, or it could be that you've exhausted your training solutions and believe it is the bit that is causing the problem.

Horses are individuals with very different tastes. In your experimentation, always begin with the softest, gentlest bit you can find. That will probably be some kind of double-jointed or flexible mullen mouth snaffle. A horse may respond immediately to a change in bit. Don't be fooled. Anything new in a horse's mouth will cause him to pay more attention. The real test is after he's been wearing it for several weeks or even months. If the behavior returns, you might try another option, depending on what problem you're trying to solve. What follows are some examples of problems or situations and some possible bitting solutions. These should be

You can often see a horse opening and closing his mouth when a rider is using a bit incorrectly or has not offered the horse any release from pressure.

considered guidelines, or starting points, rather than rules because it's impossible to recommend a bit without seeing a horse at work in his bridle, looking in his mouth, and knowing how the horse is ridden.

ENGLISH BITTING ISSUES

For the Young Horse

Whether you're building up his confidence, teaching him to accept the bit for the very first time, or refining his steering ability, take special care with young horses. After all, they're a bit like elephants: they never forget bad experiences. If you're not a confident rider and trainer, get help with your young horse.

Young horses need help understanding what rein pressure means. A solid-cheek snaffle bit, such as a full cheek, will help the horse figure out direct rein pressure. Pull on the right rein and the cheek piece puts pressure on the left cheek, so the horse's head turns, which encourages him to step over and across with his front left leg and turn right. The full cheek's design means you won't risk pulling the bit through his mouth if he's a little resistant, or pinching his lip with the sliding loose ring. It's also a little more stable, with less vertical movement than a loose ring. The stability of a solid cheek makes the young horse feel more comfortable and secure in the bit. Always use keepers to prevent the tops of a full cheek from poking you, your clothes, or your horse's nose.

For mouthpieces, a double-jointed bit with a lozenge, or other bit with a soft middle section is a good first choice. Because of the way this mouthpiece drapes across the tongue, it's very comfortable and unobtrusive for a young horse, yet provides enough gentle pressure to persuade the horse to follow the contact.

Young, Forward-Going Horse

Some horses have natural "go." They're impatient or alpha-type horses who would prefer to take charge of the situation. For a horse like this, you might need a little more reinforcement from the bit until the horse

141

Inspect your bits carefully. This Happy Mouth has a plastic burr that's in unfortunate contact with the tongue.

142

truly understands your signals and obeys them. A slightly sharper mouthpiece, such as one that adds just a little more pressure on either the tongue or the bars, may be a good solution for the sharper horse. The pressure from the reins should be soft and quick, with an immediate release. A French link mouthpiece and a solid cheek, such as an eggbutt, might be a good combination. Because the cheek piece is solid, the action of the reins is immediate, with little play in the mouthpiece. The French link has an infinitesimal amount more bite to it than a bit with a smoothly rounded lozenge.

The Dr. Bristol, which has a longer plate that's angled to press its edge against the top of the tongue when the rein is engaged, might be another option, particularly for a horse that pushes against the bit and takes control. The edge of the plate pushes on the tongue as the horse surges forward. A quick correction and then release may lighten the horse in the bridle. Once he understands not to push his tongue against the bit as a way of regaining control, you can return

to a softer option, such as a French link or lozenge-style bit.

If a young horse develops a pull, or begins to root at the bit, consider first making a change to something thinner. A thinner bit has a sharper contact with the tongue and the bars. While it may be tempting to use a solid mouth bit, such as a ported bit, the solidity of the mouthpiece leaves very little room for the younger horse to develop jaw flexibility. A solid mouth bit will also encourage him to lean or even grab the bit. Better to stick with a thinner jointed bit or something with a different middle link to see if you can solve the problem that way. Of course, it will help to work on training the horse to listen to your seat, rather than pulling back against a horse that pulls against you. Instead, create a solid place with your quiet hands and firm midsection against which he'll bump when he pulls.

Unconfident in the Bridle or Highly Sensitive Mouth

There are many horses that start out going just fine in a snaffle, and somewhere along the way they begin to drop the bit and bring their heads behind the vertical line. While they may still be trotting, the rider has lost the connection with the horse's mouth and he's curled up behind the contact. There could be several issues at work here, and again we urge you to work through the checklist of problems including not riding the horse "in front of the leg," meaning he is not responding to and moving forward from your leg aids. This problem could also be caused by saddle fit or back soreness. Most important, however, is to ride the horse forward to a giving hand. If he's still behind the bit despite help from a professional and a thorough evaluation, you might try a soft, solid bit, like a rubber or vulcanite mullen mouth.

The shape of the mullen mouthpiece leaves room for the horse's tongue, but the solid mouthpiece gives him something substantial in his mouth to help him build more confidence in the contact. The rubber mullen mouth is a very soft bit that is generally good for horses with extremely sensitive mouths.

Another option for those sensitive types is the Happy Mouth, or other polyurethane bit. The plastic coating softens the effect of the metal core, is thicker than metal, and, in some cases can be flavored to encourage the finicky horse to accept the bit. The rubber and plastic or poly bits, are thick. A horse with a small mouth or a thick tongue may not like such a thick bit.

A third possibility is a slightly ported, solid-mouthed bit, such as a lightweight ported snaffle. With room for the tongue, the solid mouthpiece distributes the pressure across the mouth like the mullen mouth bit. While neither of these has much lateral play, you can switch back to a flexible bit after the horse has learned to comfortably accept the contact.

Trained, Forward-Going Horse who Throws his Head Up When Excited

Whether you're just out for a trail ride or tackling a cross-country course, sometimes you need to remind your horse to keep his head down and his wits about him. When a horse throw his head up, it's much harder to control him. He loses his visual focus and becomes hollow and rigid through the back and the neck. It's crucial for jumping riders, and others whose horses have this habit, to work on balance with a gentle, simple bit. Still, sometimes you need a little reminder.

In this situation, you'd want a bit that applies poll pressure to encourage the horse to flex over his poll and use his topline more effectively. A good option, particularly for a horse that may not need this reminder all the time, is a Pelham bit with double reins. The rider can use the snaffle rein most of the time. By engaging the leverage rein, he can ask for poll flexion and balance when he needs it. The rider can add a delta or converter that makes the curb and the snaffle operate as one rein, and by changing his hand position he can further engage the curb action. In this case, the Pelham should have a solid mouthpiece.

Another option for the high-headed hot horse is the Kimberwicke. Using a Kimberwicke without slots allows the rein to slide on the D, giving the horse a little warning before the poll pressure is fully engaged. The uxeter with slotted reins allows the rider to adjust the reins for a little more leverage, which might be useful for days when the horse feels hotter than normal. The Kimberwicke makes a very good step-up option when the horse isn't responding to a thinner, stronger snaffle bit.

143

Trained Horse Who Gets Exuberant but Too Low in the Poll

A horse who is carrying himself properly will have his head softly in line with his neck and his poll raised slightly. He'll be carrying his head in a balanced position with his eyes forward and focused. Some horses, however, tend to drop their heads between their knees, or run "downhill" and hang on the bit. In either case, a gag bit will help lift the horse's head while at the same time encouraging him to flex at the poll. Gags are useful for cross country, the jumper ring, and the hunt field, as they help a horse who may have gotten tired to lift off his forehand and gallop more uphill. The dual actions of the gag—lifting the bit in the mouth and applying poll pressure to remind the horse to balance—are quite useful but also severe. A gag is not a beginner's bit.

Heavy Horse

Some horses may not be particularly forward or difficult to control when they get excited; they may just be heavy in the bridle. We call horses like this "on the forehand." They travel with their heads and necks below the withers and with no self-carriage.

A properly trained horse should not feel like your reins are holding him up. It's likely that the heavy horse has been made that way by poor training and poor riding, such as a "water-skier." This rider uses his hands to balance and has not ridden the horse forward from his hindquarters.

Besides retraining both rider and horse, consider a bit that encourages the horse to carry himself. Any bit with a very flexible mouthpiece, such as a double-jointed snaffle or a Waterford will have the desired effect. These bits won't work well if your horse is both on the forehand and very strong. They're very good for horses that just want you to do the work of holding up their heads and aren't balancing properly. The rollers should be tightly constructed, because otherwise they could pinch the tongue and lips and cause a new set of problems. You can use the Waterford bit as a temporary tool to aid your retraining process, not as a permanent solution. Also, Waterfords and many bits with rollers in the mouthpiece are illegal in competition dressage.

WESTERN BITTING ISSUES

The Western horse's bit is a tool to be used to add finesse. If the horse has the right foundation—he yields to pressure by softening his jaw and poll, balancing, and carrying himself—the bit becomes only a matter of the horse's personal taste.

Horse with a Locked or Tight Jaw

Ideally, the Western horse has a soft mouth and a flexible jaw. Most show ring judges prefer not to see gobs of white saliva or a very busy mouth but want to see a soft, gentle lip and relaxed mouth. A horse with a locked jaw isn't listening to subtle signals as well as he could be. Switching to a bit made of a different material, such as sweet iron, which many horses like, could increase chewing and softness. You could also try a steel bit with copper inlays, or some other combination of textures and tastes. If you're riding in a fixed-jaw bit, switch to one with a loose jaw for more lateral play in the bit. The bit will have a little more mobility in the horse's mouth and the rider will have the option of adding direct rein.

Horse Annoyed by Tongue Pressure

With such a variety of port styles available today, the horse that doesn't like tongue pressure has plenty of options. Look to a correction bit—with a high and wide curved port—for maximum tongue relief. Another option is a mullen mouth. For a well-trained horse already working in a curb bit, you might try a mechanical hackamore with a wide leather noseband to get rid of tongue pressure altogether.

Young Horse Moving to his First Curb

For horses that are still perfecting their neck reining technique, it's vital that there be some play in the shanks. A loose-jawed curb bit allows the rider to use both a direct rein for steering and a little bit of leverage action for the correct placement of the poll. You can ride with two hands, while still asking for the proper head set. If your horse hasn't yet learned to yield properly or to rate, however, you should go back to the snaffle and perfect his reining and balance.

Horse that Pokes his Nose Out

Consider this rule of thumb, from bit maker and expert Greg Darnall as told to *Western Horseman* magazine: "The heavier the bit, the more uncomfortable for the horse to have his head in any but the proper position." So if your horse has a tendency to poke his nose in front of the vertical, choose a heavier version of your current bit as a first step to fixing this problem. The heavier the bit, the more encouragement the horse will feel to bring his nose in. Consider this: which is more difficult, holding your arm out in front of you while carrying a five-pound weight, or bringing it closer to your body? Hence the theory that using a heavier bit will encourage a horse to bring his head closer to the vertical.

Horse Doesn't Steer Well

If you're experienced enough to start a young horse by yourself, the bit of choice is definitely some kind of full cheek snaffle. Many trainers, from Western to racehorse, prefer this bit for a very first bitting attempt. Variations on the full cheek can be found with different mouthpieces, with some trainers preferring the sweet iron jointed bits to promote softness and others preferring a bit with some kind of "keys" that hang on the horse's tongue and encourage him to chew.

Rider Who is Not Quiet with Her Hands

Here's a common scenario: a rider comes to a trainer with a horse that the rider says is hard to control.

145

Here's how the scenario plays out: Rider buys a horse. He may be a little "too much horse" for the rider. Perhaps the horse is a little green or a little hot. The rider takes a hold of the reins and, because of her own anxiety, begins to hang on the horse's mouth, never offering the horse any relief from pressure. She may, additionally, ride the horse backwards—which means that she rides with a pulling hand instead of a following hand.

At this point, the horse's anxiety level increases every time the rider gets on. Pull, pull, pull. The more the rider pulls, the more the horse feels constrained and anxious. Guess what happens next? He either fights the contact by throwing his head up and down or rooting into the bit (which is a very clear signal from rider to horse: "*Let go!*") or his flight instinct kicks in and he runs *through* the bit.

The rider begins to worry that the horse might run away with her. So she goes to the local feed store and asks for a stronger bit. The guy at the feed store presents her with a slow twist snaffle, for example. She takes it home and puts it on, but in the meantime, she's done nothing to fix the horse's understanding of contact. She picks up the reins and the horse begins to pull, because that's how she rides. And now the horse feels even more pressure or even a bit of pain because he's got that harsh bit in his mouth.

The trainer watches the rider for a few minutes, and then retreats to the tack room to dig through her bits. She brings out a soft double-link snaffle or some other gentle bit, and gets on the horse. The trainer doesn't pull, and the horse begins to relax. So you

see, with some hard work on the rider's part to learn to trust the horse and not pull, this problem can be solved.

A horse that appears "out of control" may actually be running from a rider that has an overly harsh or heavy hand and is using an overly harsh bit. A rider that never releases the contact, or has a one-sided conversation with the horse's mouth, can actually begin to cause training problems.

146

A tongue layer can sometimes help the horse that lolls or hangs the tongue. Unfortunately this can become a habit that's very difficult to break.

147

TONGUE VICES

You cannot discuss bitting without coming across the problem of the tongue. Whether it sticks out, draws up, goes over the bit, or otherwise misbehaves, tongue vices signal discomfort. Tongue problems are so common because horses use their tongues to protect other parts of their mouths. Some started sticking out their tongues due to pain and now do it out of habit. Whatever the cause, experienced horsemen agree this is one of the trickiest problems to solve.

In many show arenas, including hunter, dressage, and some Western classes, tongue lolling is considered a serious problem and affects the final score. A horse that carries his tongue out is not soft or submissive to the bridle as required by these disciplines.

The tongue serves as a cushion, and many horses use it to protect their mouths when they are in pain. Indeed, you may actually feel the horse "rooting" or pulling downwards a second or two before the tongue emerges. His neck muscles may stiffen. His back may

◀ The author and her horse, Volare, who had a chronic tongue lolling habit.

be tight. Frequently, pain elsewhere in the body can cause the tongue to stick out.

Some horses will suck their tongues up to the back of their throats. This is one of the most detrimental tongue problems, because it can block the horse's airway. You might see this problem on the racetrack or cross-country course, but rarely with casual arena or trail work.

Other horses bring their tongues over the bit. This pretty much negates the impact of the bit and, like all tongue problems, is almost always caused by discomfort caused by the bit on the tongue.

When you've got a tongue loller, the first step is a veterinary examination of the mouth, the teeth, the back, and the neck.

Bit makers have come up with a veritable boatload of bit options to correct tongue problems. They have made bits that have a tongue depressor-type device called a "nagbut," which attaches to the center of the middle link of a double-jointed snaffle and rests on the tongue. A similar concept, although likely a more severe device, is the barmouth figure-eight with two round rings that attach at the center of the bar. The figure-eight rests on the tongue. Yet another ingenious creation is a rubber device known as a tongue layer, which wraps around the bit, pointing toward the horse's throat. Its purpose is to prevent the horse from putting his tongue over the bit.

Some snaffles have been designed with players, or little keys that rest on the horse's tongue and provide a toy for the horse to fool with instead of attempting to put his tongue over the bit. Trainers used to use these bits to start horses, the theory being that the players would encourage acceptance of the bit and loosen the horse's jaw, encouraging chewing and salivation. They've largely gone out of style and are very rare these days.

Wide ported bits and mullen mouths, which discourage the horse from putting the tongue over the bit by giving it plenty of room are sometimes a good solution. The key is to address the tongue problem as soon as you can by reinforcing basic training.

If the horse begins to put his tongue out or over the bit, have his teeth checked and re-evaluate your riding and training methods. It could be a simple fix, or it could be a habit. Rarely will changing a bit fix the tongue lolling problem.

CASE STUDIES

The Tongue Loller

The concept and execution of "submission" is perhaps most key to the bitting and tongue conundrum. Indeed, a horse who is lolling his tongue has not accepted the bit—he's trying to avoid it. That's why it's so frowned upon in equestrian sports that judge horse and rider partnership, rather than pure athleticism, such as jumpers, ropers, and barrel racers, where many successful athletes have tongue problems.

During the course of researching and writing this book, I was simultaneously starting my young Hanoverian mare toward her dressage career. My former event horse had been a chronic tongue hanger—no change of bit, noseband, or device changed that. He came with the habit and he never lost it, although he was a stellar horse in all other ways.

My second horse, however, was a blank slate. Raised from a baby and started carefully with gentle training, she moved quickly her first year, learning to stretch into the bridle and move off leg pressure. She was progressing perfectly. One day, about a year into her training, I saw a sliver of tongue begin to stick out of the left side of her mouth. Then a little more tongue, and a little more, until an inch chunk of tongue was sticking out.

What had precipitated this sudden change? The previous weekend Belle had visited a jumper trainer who had longed her around on a circle rather aggressively. She'd also been ridden by a relatively novice rider who, when trying to steer her, had pulled up harshly on the reins.

There was also the fact that she'd been quite "hard" on the left rein for quite a while—a condition caused by my very own bad riding habit of dropping my left shoulder.

Whatever the cause, I stopped all work with the bit and called the vet. Step one was a thorough mouth exam. Her teeth had been floated just six weeks prior. I doubted that was the problem. I could feel a sizable muscle knot that had developed around her third cervical vertebra—a sign of some uneven muscle development that had been

a matter of concern to me for some time. The vet found no sharp points on her teeth but he did find a small sore on the inside of her right lip and a healing laceration on her tongue.

I felt a little relief—at least there seemed to be some reason for the discomfort. Question was, now what?

I followed this course of action: First, I gave her a month off from riding with bit and bridle, to give her time to heal. This horse does not tolerate pain at all. During that month, I rode her in a rope halter and did a lot of relaxation work with her. I then borrowed a cross-under bitless bridle from a friend and rode her in that for another month. In fact, she went quite well in the bitless and I never once saw her tongue. In the bitless bridle I worked on exercises to supple her to the left and built on those by working on throughness to the bridle. I would have continued to ride her in it had she not been such a talented dressage horse. Bitless bridles are not yet legal for competition.

Next, I opened my tack trunk full of forgotten bits:

- Single-link, level 2 Myler
- Vulcanite mullen mouth
- French link hollow mouth
- KK Ultra
- Sprenger Tournado
- Double-jointed KK with a copper lozenge
- Steel, eggbutt single-link snaffle in a medium width

- Full-cheek single-link snaffle
- D-ring rubber single-link snaffle
- Baucher
- Single-link Happy Mouth
- Copper and steel mullen mouth

I tried the Tournado, which claims to help tongue problems, but she immediately opened her mouth and argued with that bit. The vulcanite mullen mouth was much too thick for her delicate mouth. The Sprenger with the Aurigan lozenge was too thin, although it and the French link seem to give her about the same amount of comfort. In the end, I opted for the hollow mouth French link to restart her.

I put her on the longe line with side reins—no tongue. I rode her on a loose rein at the walk with the bit on. I switched to the bitless for any more intense work.

The only way to solve any bitting problem is to be creative about it. In this case, we suspected pain—whether from the tongue itself, from the neck, or from the back. Because the incident had been precipitated by a couple of difficult rides, I suspected something was hurting her; she'd never shown her tongue in the past. Starting her back slowly, riding her forward and correctly into the bridle, and plying her with peppermints so she learned to associate the bit with good things rather than pain were some of our tactics in getting her to accept the bit once again.

After two months of riding Belle in a bitless bridle, riding her forward, and asking her to accept the bit, the tongue problem is now quite a bit better. We've developed a method where, when I see her tongue, I drive her into my right rein with my left leg and gently lift my left hand. When her tongue slides in I tell her she's a good girl and rub her neck with my left hand. The tongue pops out now and then still, but it's almost always precipitated by a feeling that she's locked in the left neck rather than traveling straight between the reins. When I correct this problem, I don't see her tongue.

There is a serious effort on my part to ride her with the utmost correctness, carrying a very soft feel, riding her from back to front so she engages her hindquarters and uses her neck and topline correctly. Most importantly, I worked diligently on the correctness of the left bend and engagement of the left hind leg.

Overall, such a focus on proper training, plus allowing her time to heal from her injury, and acknowledging overall that she is a very sensitive horse and not at all stoic when it comes to pain, allowed me to think analytically and problem-solve around her particular problem.

The Event Horse

Nancy Ambrosiano is an experienced event rider and the coach of the Los Alamos, New Mexico Pony Club. She has a collection of about forty bits—antique, new, variations on a theme—that she uses in her pony club classes. With so many choices, you would think that she'd have a bit in her collection that would work on her off-the-track thoroughbred event horse.

"Stretch" is a high-strung, forward-going former racehorse that does not appreciate pressure on his mouth. In fact, the horse is quite sensitive and would tend to panic when Nancy, galloping toward a cross-country fence, would half halt and hold any kind of pressure on his mouth.

"Stretch is all adrenaline. He also has a temper and when he got upset he would flip his head and run to the fence with his nose inverted. He would panic when he ran into the bit," Nancy describes. With such a variety of bits to choose from, Nancy tried everything from a soft, synthetic dog bone to a Pelham to a Kimberwicke, with no success.

She also went through a period of serious retraining, working on smaller fences, gymnastics, and dressage to try to teach Stretch to accept the bit and half halt without panicking.

His behavior improved a little, but he still had a tendency to panic when Nancy used rein pressure in combination with a balancing seat to ask Stretch to sit back on his hindquarters and balance before the jump.

She came across a Myler combination bit. The Myler combination bit is a bubble bit— otherwise known as a Pessoa or a European gag, which has several unique features. First, the bit includes a hackamore-style noseband attached with parachute cord to the curb strap, a barrel snaffle that disperses the pressure across the tongue, and the gag option of the Pessoa.

Attach the reins to the largest ring and the bit becomes a regular Myler barrel mouth snaffle with a little leverage, thanks to a ring stop that prevents the reins from moving freely on the ring. Once the reins stop, hackamore-style pressure is engaged on the noseband. This allows the horse to carry the bit in his mouth with very little pressure, but also allows the rider to engage a relatively strong half halt through the use of the hackamore. The canons of the bit are angled to relieve tongue pressure. Attaching the reins to either of the rings below the snaffle adds leverage.

For Stretch, a horse that feared mouth pressure, the hackamore option allowed Nancy to use minimal pressure on the bit while still reminding the horse to sit up and balance back on his hindquarters. Using moderate weight in her hands and a very quick half halt, she's now able to control Stretch's forward-going nature and use his athleticism to gallop safely and correctly to both cross-country and stadium jumps.

Nancy's pony club coaching experience exposed her to numerous examples that serve as good lessons in appropriate bitting. For example, she cites an event horse she sold to a nearby pony club participant. When she sold the horse she warned the new owner that she always rode the horse in a Kimberwicke, yet she failed to specify precisely what kind of mouthpiece the Kimberwicke had.

The next time Nancy saw this young girl riding her new horse, she was flying willy-nilly around an arena, without a lot of steering or brakes. Confused by the formerly well-behaved and well-trained horse's behavior, Nancy investigated. Turns out, the child did have a Kimberwicke in the horse's mouth, but it was a jointed bit—meaning the child had very little lateral control, even though she had the seemingly stronger leverage bit in the horse's mouth.

This example reminds us of the importance of a holistic approach to bitting. Case in point: Nancy fit her daughter's horse with a solid-core mullen mouth Pelham— it's a good bit for a horse that tends to get strong cross country but doesn't need a lot of correction to bring him back to a sensible balance. In a rush before an event, Nancy picked up the wrong bit, choosing instead a rubber mullen mouth with a wire core instead. This slight change in an otherwise identical bit makes a huge difference. It turns a solid, stiff bit into an incredibly flexible one.

Later, when Nancy's daughter was on the cross-country course, she heard her daughter's repeated pleas of "Whoa, whoa, whoa," as she galloped around. Her daughter managed to complete her course without an accident, but it wasn't until after the event that Nancy realized her mistake: the wire core mullen mouth was so flexible it provided no "barrier" into which her petite daughter could reinforce her half halts on the cross-country course.

The Colt Starter

Joe Fernandez, who starts horses of all kinds, has learned a lot of different methods and developed his own style of starting horses. Part natural horsemanship, part old cowboy (Joe's family has been starting colts for a hundred years in Mora, New Mexico), Joe has attached his full-cheek, single-jointed snaffle to a rope that slips over the horse's head like a headstall, but has knots like a rope halter. The horse, Joe explains, feels the pressure from the knots just as he would in a plain rope halter, but also feels the cheek pieces of the full-cheek on the sides of his mouth. That action truly encourages the horse to turn.

Acclimating horses to the bit requires nothing more than a little patience, a soft touch, and some gentle encouragement, Joe says. It helps if the trainer has warmed the bit up before putting it in the horse's mouth, especially if the weather is chilly. To do this, simply roll the bit back and forth in your palms. Gently insert your thumb into the horse's mouth and press down on the bar while holding the rest of the bridle on the opposite side of the horse's head. Make sure the bridle is neither too tight nor too loose— you want the horse to feel comfortable with the bit right away. When he opens his mouth, gently slide the bridle up towards his ears while supporting the bit with your thumb and forefinger. Then adjust the bridle correctly. Some trainers like to give the horse a sugar cube or a peppermint at this point, to encourage the horse to chew on the bit, and to signify that bitting is a happy, tasty experience. The horse may do funny things with his mouth—he may yawn or open his jaws and slide them side to side. He may stick out his tongue or suck on the bit. Whatever the case, just let him stand there and get used to it. Some trainers also like to keep the halter on underneath the bridle with an attached lead rope, so they can control the horse without putting any pressure on the bit. Above all, the horse needs to have a positive, pleasant first bitting experience. There's no need to leave the bit in his mouth for a long period of time. Gradually increasing the time and adding activities, such as leading and stopping, will habituate your horse to the bit quickly and easily.

English to Western

Trainer Julie Goodnight tells of a student who was switching from English to Western. The student purchased a mature, seasoned, and well-trained Western horse taught to work in a curb, with a very loose rein. He had been ridden softly and with one hand.

In English riding, riders are taught to take a "feel" of the horse's mouth. Sometimes that feel is just a few ounces of pressure between the bit and the hands. Other times it may be more intense. After all, we want our horses working into the bridle, pushing from back to front. English riders use a snaffle bit for the most part—it is designed to carry the pressure of the hands and spread it across the horse's tongue, bars, and lips.

This rider, who knew very little about Western riding, believed the curb bit that the horse came with was too severe, so she changed to a snaffle, as she would have done with an English-trained horse. This rider was under the impression she was being more humane by putting what she perceived as a gentler bit in her horse's mouth.

Only it wasn't. Not for this horse, anyway. And not with this particular rider. The rider took "contact" as she would with a dressage horse or hunter, and the horse became braced in her back in an effort to protect her mouth from the rider's constant contact. Goodnight switched bits—changing from a straight snaffle to a hybrid bit (a Myler) with a hackamore-style noseband, a bit, and chin and poll pressure. Using this combination bit distributed the pressure from the horse's mouth to several different points on her head. Over time and with some careful instruction, the horse began to lighten up. The rider was able to work with her instructor to develop more Western-style hands and rein contact. She also began to understand what was too much pressure and what was just the right amount. Over time, the rider was able to go back to the curb bit. That made the horse much more comfortable.

Western to Dressage

Lori Brookins, an Arizona-based dressage rider, switched her horse from Western to dressage. Before she bought her current horse, she tried him several times, and noted that he was light as a feather. Upon further inspection, she noted that the bit he was wearing was a fast-twist, rusty copper snaffle. She also noticed that he had a nasty sore in the corner of his left lip.

As a dressage rider, Brookins changed him to a double-jointed loose ring snaffle with a bean in the middle. He still had that nasty sore in the left corner of his mouth. Brookins admits to a "terrible lopsidedness in that I always take up a tad bit more right rein than left." Could that have been the cause of the sore? It's possible that Brookins was inadvertently pulling the bit through the horse's mouth, causing a left side sore to develop. The cause of the sore was somewhat mysterious, but she solved

153

the problem by changing the horse to an eggbutt snaffle, although he remained heavy in her hands. A second option was a KK bit, with an angled bead in the center.

In the long run, Brookins' problem with her Appaloosa might have been quite similar to the one Julie Goodnight described. Brookins' horse had been a Western horse, and although he was ridden in what is considered a harsh bit, he was light because he'd learned to carry himself. During retraining, Brookins learned an important lesson—that it's really not the bit that matters. The most important element is proper training. "If he is in self carriage, and as uphill as a horse like him can physically carry himself, he is happy."

CHAPTER - 12

BITTING MYTHS AND TRUTHS

Bitting is part of every horseman's life. It can also be quite expensive, since it is the rare tack store that will loan a rider a bit just to try (once a bit has been in a horse's mouth it is generally scratched and cannot be sold as new).

At first blush, bitting seems a vast and complicated issue. It takes knowledge, patience, and perseverance to navigate the bit aisle of the tack store and figure out how to help our horses. Even so, it can also be surprisingly simple. Several of the trainers interviewed for this book noted that they often look like heroes when they change a horse's bit and instantly solve what seemed to the rider to be a highly complicated problem.

Here, we summarize the most common myths and truths about bits.

MYTHS AND MISCONCEPTIONS

1) **A Western curb bit is a harsh bit.** Yes, in the wrong hands, it is. But in Western riding the horse is trained well enough that he can be ridden very lightly, with just the shifting weight of the reins to guide or remind him. This is particularly true for bits with longer shanks— the dangling rein on the long shanks definitely creates some sensation in the horse's most sensitive mouth.

2) **One of the most common misconceptions in the bitting world is that a ported bit is a curb or leverage bit.** Not so. There are many snaffles with ports.

3) **If you need a stronger bit, switch to a curb.** In fact, curbs are advanced bits for well-trained horses, not disobedient horses. That's why advanced Western bridle horses and high-level dressage horses can carry a curb bit—both types of bits require highly skilled rider and horse response. They aren't meant to shout louder at unresponsive horses.

4) **Jointed bits are always softer than straight bar bits.** Not always true! Mullen mouths, Myler bits, and some wide-ported bits can be gentler for horses than jointed bits. It depends on what kind of lateral flexibility you need and how

your horse feels about bar pressure rather than tongue and lip pressure.

5) **The Tom Thumb is a good transition bit to use when you're moving from a snaffle to a curb.** Nothing could be further from the truth. The Tom Thumb may look like a "snaffle" bit because it is jointed in the center. But it isn't one. A true snaffle has direct contact, with the reins connecting directly to the bit. So if you pull on the left rein, it pulls the horse's head to the left. With the Tom Thumb, however, the reins are attached to the shanks. If you attempt to direct-rein the horse to the left, you're actually applying leverage, rather than asking him to turn left. You're also exacerbating the nutcracker effect of the single-jointed mouthpiece. If you pull back on the horse's mouth with both reins, the shanks engage leverage and the joint in the center of the bit folds over the horse's tongue, presses on the bars, and may even poke the roof of his mouth. Add the leverage effect of the shanks (remember how those shanks add triple the pounds per square inch?) and you're basically asking the horse to bring his head down, while at the same time poking him in the roof of the mouth when he does. And, with the curb chain added to this combination, you've made it nearly impossible for the horse to yield to pressure.

On the English side, a similarly ineffective bitting combination is the jointed Pelham or any other kind of jointed curb. While it may seem like a softer bit because of the joint, in fact it's relatively ineffective for any of the purposes people think these bits are good for. It's not a particularly soft bit because it has that nutcracker action, nor is it particularly effective as a curb bit because it will cause the horse to want to evade the leverage action. A better option, for both English and Western, is to perfect the basics of training as much as possible *before* moving to a curb bit. If a horse doesn't turn, is heavy in the hands, or is running off with the rider, then a big step back to basics is the first step, not a leverage bit with a jointed mouthpiece.

6) **Pull back on the reins to stop a horse.** Unfortunately, many of us learned to ride in the "kick to go, pull to stop" school of equitation. The seat and the leg signal the "whoa" while the hand closes on the reins. The bit is neither the horse's brakes nor his steering wheel, although they can be used that way when necessary to reinforce the other aids.

7) **A linked bit is a snaffle.** Not so! A linked bit with leverage cheeks is a leverage bit, not a snaffle.

8) **Buying a new bit will solve your problems.** As Julie Goodnight said earlier in this book, you cannot buy your way out of a training problem. Experiment, train, get help, but realize that the actual bit is a very small part of a very large overall horse management picture.

As you go forth into your bitting experiments, remember to look holistically at your horse, your riding, and your bit to

157

determine your next steps. A bit is only as good as the hands to which it is attached, so make becoming a better rider your first priority. Think empathetically about your horse's mouth and work to quiet your bouncy hands and soften your contact. You might be surprised at how much money you'll save just by having a friend longe you without stirrups or reins, or by spending 20 minutes riding without stirrups every day to improve your balance. Look at your horse's training issues from a number of different angles, starting with the training of the horse and the habits of the rider and moving on to the equipment. Sometimes, it's a combination of all three that solves the problem.

The world of bits and bitting is full of misconceptions and misinformation. We hope that after reading this book, some of those myths have been debunked and you're better able to make the right choices for your horses.

159

GLOSSARY

Action: The combined pressure that the bit places on the tongue, the bars, the lips, and the poll.

Balance: (1) The physical properties of a bit, such as whether each canon is the same weight; (2) how the bit rests in the horse's mouth and moves with the application of a leverage rein.

Bar mouth: A single piece of metal that forms the mouthpiece of a bit.

Bars: The space along the gums in the horse's mouth between the front incisors (or tushes) and the molars. Sometimes called the "interdental space."

Baucher: Created by controversial French dressage master François Baucher, this bit is technically a snaffle. The bit hangs in the mouth from the bridle rings and offers a small amount of poll pressure. The distance between the bridle rings and the mouthpiece creates a very slight leverage effect.

Bicycle chain: A serrated, hinged mouthpiece that is quite severe, now mostly used on mules, although it has fallen out of fashion.

Canon: The piece of the mouthpiece that runs from cheek piece or ring to the center.

Cheek: Either the rings or the shanks that attach the bit to the bridle and the reins.

Cheek pieces: (1) The leather or rope pieces of the bridle that run along the horse's cheek bone and attach to the bit; (2) the metal rings or shanks that attach the bridle and the reins to the mouthpiece of a snaffle bit. The word is used synonymously with "cheek."

Correction: A high, wide port that allows room for the tongue. Its straight canons apply pressure to the bars.

Cricket: A copper roller, often textured, found in between the arms of a port.

Curb: Any of the leverage bits that have shanks and a curb chain or strap. Because of the distance between the mouthpiece and the bridle rings, as well as the length of the shank and the action of the chain or strap, curb mouthpieces serve as a fulcrum in the horse's mouth.

Curb chain: The metal chain that sits in the chin groove and is engaged when a rider puts pressure on the shanks of a leverage bit.

Curb strap: The leather strap that sits in the chin groove and engages when the rider takes contact with the shanks of a leverage bit.

Dick Christian: A mouthpiece that is similar to the Dr. Bristol, but has a ring instead of a plate in the center link.

D-ring or dee ring: A cheek that has a flat side next to the horse's cheek and a rounded ring. The flat side prevents the bit from sliding through the horse's mouth. It is useful for horses that need extra encouragement in steering.

Dr. Bristol: A double-linked mouthpiece with a plate in the center. The edge of the plate presses against the horse's tongue when rein pressure is applied.

Double-jointed: A bit with two joints connecting the canons with a center link, lozenge, plate, or ring.

Eggbutt: A snaffle with flattened rings and a mouthpiece that is connected with two cylinders that serve as hinges. The canons are wider next to the rings, and taper down toward the center. The ring is egg-shaped.

Fiador: The throatlatch and knot that connects the mecate rein with the rest of a rope hackamore. Sometimes pronounced as "Theodore."

French link: A double-jointed bit with a dog bone or figure-eight-shaped link in the center.

Hackamore: Also called a nose bridle, a hackamore has no bit. It controls the horse through pressure on the poll and the nose. It is derived from the bitless halters in which early Spanish equestrians trained their young horses.

Hyoid bone: The apparatus in the horse's skull to which the tongue is attached. A key structure involved in poll flexion created by pressure on the bit and reins.

Kimberwicke or Kimblewicke: With bit rings shaped like an eggbutt, the Kimberwicke has a curb chain that applies a small amount of leverage.

Jointed: A mouthpiece with a single or double link that joins the canons in the center.

Leverage: The ratio of rein tension to poll and curb chain or strap pressure. The ratio is determined by the total length of the shank and the distance from the rein ring to the mouthpiece. A 1-inch purchase and a 4-inch total shank produce a ratio of 1:3.

Leverage bit: An indirect contact bit to which reins are attached below the mouthpiece. Pressure on the reins pulls the bridle rings down, tightens the curb strap (if there is one), and swivels the bit forward in the horse's mouth.

Loriner or lorimer: An archaic word for an individual who makes bits, spurs, and other metal tack for horses. The word is still used in the United Kingdom.

Mecate (pronounced me-cot-ee and sometimes called McCarty): A rope traditionally made from twisted mane hair. Usually 22 feet in length, the mecate is used both as the reins and as a lead rope.

Pelham: An English bit with the option of two reins. One is for snaffle control and one for curb leverage. Commonly used for hunters and jumpers.

Mullen mouth: A slightly arched, single-bar bit. It is considered a gentle bit because it provides ample room for the horse's tongue.

Nathe: A polyurethane compound created in Germany and used in the mouthpieces of bits. Nathe bits often have a metal core.

Port: The inverted "U" found in single-bar bits. It provides space for the horse's

161

tongue, but can also make unwanted contact with the roof of his mouth if not used properly.

Purchase: The section of the shank from the mouthpiece to the bridle ring. The length of the purchase and the length of the lower shank determine a bit's severity. A long lower shank with a short purchase increases the severity of the leverage action.

Romal rein: A heavy rein used with a shanked bit. A slight shift of the rein is often sufficient to achieve the desired reaction from the horse.

Shank: The cheek piece of a leverage bit, attached to the canon and running from bridle ring to rein ring.

Signal: In a bit with rings, the slight delay in rein action as the rein slides on the ring.

Single-jointed: A mouthpiece with two canons and a single joint.

Snaffle: A direct-contact bit.

Spade: A vaquero-style bit with a straight bar, and a high narrow port with a cricket. Considered an advanced bit for both horse and rider.

Trigeminal nerve: This nerve originates at the horse's pharynx, splits into three branches (hence *trigeminal*), and follows the length of the mouth on both top and bottom of the jaw. It is "command central" for the sensations the horse feels on his head.

Vulcanite: A hardened rubber used for bits.

BIBLIOGRAPHY

Anthony, David, Dimitri Telegin, and Dorcas Brown. "The Origin of Horseback Riding," *Scientific American* (December 1991): 94–100.

Anthony, David and Dorcas Brown. "The Eneolithic Horse Exploitation in the Eurasian Steppes: Diet, Ritual and Riding." *Antiquity* 74 (2000): 75–86.

Clark, John. *The Medieval Horse and His Equipment*. Museum of London monograph, 2004.

Cook, Robert, PhD, FRCVS. *Metal in the Mouth, The Abusive Effects of Bitted Bridles.* Robert Cook, 2003.

Cook, Jeff. "The ABCs of Bits and Bitting." *Practical Horseman* (March 2004): 60–65.

de la Boisselière, Eliane and Guy de la Boisselière. *Eperonnerie et parure du cheval de l'Antiquité à nos jours.* Racine, 2004.

Edwards, Elwyn Hartley. *The Complete Book of Bits and Bitting*. London: David and Charles, 2004.

Gleche, Jon. M. "Oral Examination of the Horse." *The Horse* (February 1, 2007): #8818 from www.thehorse.com.

Gurney, Hilda. "Contact, the Third Element of the Training Scale." *Dressage Today* (November 2008): 20–21.

Harman, Joyce, DVM. *Anatomy and Physiology of the Mouth as it Relates to Bits*. Myler Company, www.myler.com.

Hecox, Ross. "If the Bit Fits." *Western Horseman* (May 2007): 70–76.

Kapitzke, Gerhard. *The Bit and the Reins: Developing Good Contact and Sensitive Hands*. North Pomfret Vt.: Trafalgar Square Publishing, 2004.

Latchford, Benjamin. *The Loriner*. London: Nichols, Son and Co., 1871.

Malm, Gerhard A. *Bits and Bridles, An Encyclopedia*. Valley Falls, Kansas: Grasshopper Publishers, 1996.

Manfredi, J., H. M. Clayton, and F. J. Derksen. "Effects of different bits and bridles on the frequency of induced swallowing in cantering horses." *Equine and Comparative Exercise Physiology* (2005): 2:241–244.

Mangum, A. J. "Selecting Bits and Spurs." *Western Horseman* (June 2002): 105–108.

Roberts, Tom. *Horse Control and the Bit*. T. A. and P. R. Roberts, 1969.

Smith, Devereaux Fran, Darnell, Greg. *A Bit of Information,* Western Horseman Booklet.

163

Jahiel, Jessica. *Choosing the Right Bit for Your Horse*. Storey Publishing, 2001.

Miller, Robert M. *Natural Horsemanship Explained*. Guilford, Ct.: The Lyons Press, 2007.

Schulte, Brigitte and Heinz Baumann. *Leading with Feeling*, second edition. Herm Sprenger Company, 2007.

Strickland, Charlene. "Protect Your Horse's Mouth." *The Horse* (October 1, 1998): #561 from www.thehorse.com.

Taylor, Louis. *Bits: Their History, Use and Misuse*. New York: Harper and Row, First Edition, 1966.

Vernon, Hilary. *The Allen Illustrated Guide to Bits and Bitting*. London: J. A. Allen Co., 1998.

Webber, Toni. *Mouths and Bits*. Kenilworth Press, 1990.

Xenophon. *The Art of Horsemanship* (Morgan, Morris H., editor and translator). Mineola, NY: Dover Publications, 2006.

Engelke, Elisabeth and Gasse, Hagen. *Zur Lage unterschiedlicher Trensengebisse im Pferdemail*. Hannover, Germany: Anatomishces Institut, Tierarztliche Hochschule, 2002.

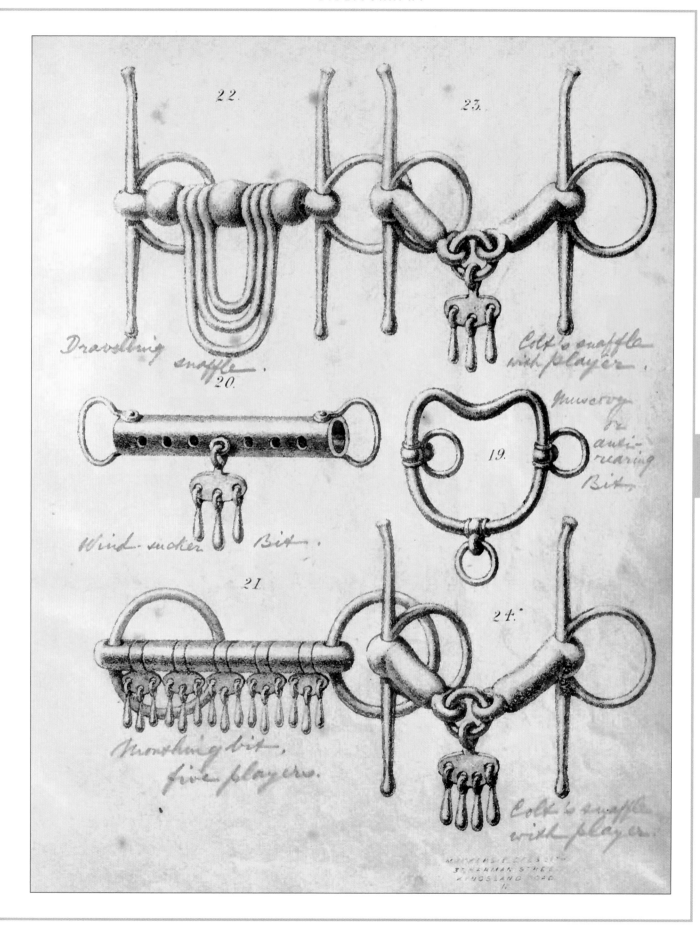